DIRECT MARKETING 101

FOR

DIRECT SALES PEOPLE

AND

DIRECT SALES BUSINESS OWNERS

WRITTEN BY

WAYNE E. SHILLUM

DEDICATION

THIS BOOK IS DEDICATED TO

MY BROTHER-IN-LAW

A. GRANT LEE, B.A., M.A., CPM

THANKS FOR ALL YOUR HELP
OVER THE YEARS

Authors Comments

Most studies conducted to find out what makes a company succeed or fail; stated that one of the main reasons for failure was the lack of a good business plan or marketing plan.

At the same time, they indicated that one of the main reasons for success was having a good business plan and marketing plan. Therefore, one of the first things that any bank or lending institution will ask for when you need assistance, is your business and marketing plans.

Table of Contents

ACKNOWLEDGMENTS

Our Research consisted of the following Sources:

1. Industry Canada – Small Business Research and Statistics

2. Government of Canada – Canadian Business Network

3. Government of Canada – Services for Entrepreneurs

4. Research on Small Business report

5. Statistics Canada

6. SBA – Small Business Administration

7. Dun & Bradstreet

8. Chartered Banks

9. Wikipedia

10. A. Grant Lee B.A., M.A., CPM - AGL Marketing Limited

After reviewing the information from the above sources, we then summarized what we found, and we put together the information found on the following pages.

WHO IS THIS WRITTEN FOR?

This book is NOT written for the Advanced Marketer

It is written for those who may find themselves looking for ways to stabilize or expand their business through marketing and sales. Marketing is essential to increase leads and customers and build sustainability for sales people and companies alike.

Most new businesses do not have a marketing plan because they start with some existing business to get them going. Very often it takes a while before it becomes obvious that something is preventing the business from expanding.

In some cases, it becomes a matter of survival and the owner is saying what more can I do to ensure my future?

This book is divided into two parts.

Part one "What is Marketing" - written to establish a base for the person new to marketing. It will be their introduction to marketing, its terms, theories and concepts.

Part two "Marketing Plans" - will explain and show how to prepare and implement a Marketing Plan.

Both were inspired by my own journey and struggles that occurred during my 35 years of professional selling and marketing.

What You Will Find in this Book

In Part One - We Provide

1. A large glossary section explains the different marketing terms.

2. Marketing - Tips, Tools, Concepts, Theories, and Tactics that will prepare you for the undertaking in Part two.

Part One will provide the foundation for understanding the basics of marketing and marketing plans. It is important to know and understand these areas before you start part two.

Part Two is divided into four sections.

S1 - Information and Statistics

- Why marketing plans are essential
- What lending institutions look for as essential for a loan?

S2 - Marketing Plan Components

- You will first learn what the basic components of a marketing plan are before you begin the process of creation one.

S3 - Plan Creation

- Once you understand what the different components are we will provide a step by step process with sample questions for you to answer, to create your own outline.
- We then show you how to summarize and establish the objectives for your plan and prepare your final draft.
- The greatest benefit in putting your own marketing plan together, is that you will find it necessary to look at all the aspects that will make your business successful.

S4 - Plan Implementation

- The final part of the process is taking your plan and showing you how to put it into operation.

A company without a marketing plan is like a ship without a rudder traveling in circles hoping to discover the catch of the day.

Without a marketing plan, there is no destination or a pathway by which you can reach your goals.

PART ONE - WHAT IS MARKETING?

The Term Marketing comes from the act of going to market to buy or sell products or services. In earlier times the marketplace was the local village market "the center square" which was the hub of a town's day to day commerce.

It was the simplest form of marketing where the people who were selling, displayed their wares. The buying shoppers, searched the market place for their daily needs.

Today these markets are also found in many cities, and they are usually well attended because of the social nature involved. They are often referred to as a "farmers market" because of their high farm produce content.

Some Definitions of Marketing

a) The process used to determine what products or services may be of interest to customers and the strategy to be used in obtaining their business.

> What type of advertising will be used?
>
> What type of sales methods will be used?
>
> What types of communications will be used?

b) It is the process through which the customer is identified, their needs are determined and satisfied, and efforts are made to obtain new business and keep the customers for future transactions".

c) Marketing is the organized efforts of a business to create communicate and deliver products and services of value, to meet the needs of their target market while making a profit.

Marketing is Constantly Changing

The older versions or concepts of marketing were much easier to perform. They were simply displaying or advertising the products and services, selling them and delivering them if required.

Today, marketing has changed dramatically by including the use of psychology, sociology, economics, and social media networking, with many new forms of research and accountability referred to as analytics.

These elements are all now used to determine who the customers will be, where they are located, what their needs are, how to get their attention and how to get the sale. We can even determine when the best time of day, month or year is to get their attention for a product.

The seller is now the marketer, who is reaching out to their targeted audience to inform them of their company, their products and their services (their offerings). Marketing is the first step to enable the selling process.

The purchaser or shopper is now the one who is in search of products or services for themselves or their company. They are the consumer or end user.

The glossary in this book is only a partial list of terms used to describe marketing as it exists today. It is certainly large enough to obtain the basics for an introduction to marketing and marketing plans.

Marketing has become a more complex process with many potential vendors fighting for the attention to purchase their offerings and to keep the purchaser as a loyal repeat customer.

Companies have always relied on some type of marketing to play a key role in the building of a successful business.

It still is often done in part, by the sales department.

Here it is known as "PROSPECTING"

How We Have Evolved

Today's smarter businesses rely on a marketing department and the latest technology to reach their target markets and find prospects. This releases the sales person to develop the sale, make the presentation and close it.

The B2B (Business to Business) purchaser has adopted a new attitude. They no longer wait for sales people to visit so that they can become informed. They will not spend the time listening to boring sales presentations, when they have no immediate need for a product or service.

Opening the door at random to sales people passing by to gather information for future use has dramatically changed both sales and marketing.

B2B Purchasers have now adopted the "when needed" concept before they will spend time searching for or reviewing a product or service. In today's world, the instant availability of up to date information on products and services has removed the long information gathering process.

Purchasers now do most of their own research on the internet or select from visible products or services that are the result of someone's successful marketing campaign.

In this way, the purchaser feels that they are in control and their time is not wasted where it is not required. They also feel that they will increase their chances of finding the best product or service at the best price for their immediate need because they have better resources to do it.

They also feel that they have more control over their company's success and will have more time to perform their other tasks within the organization.

The B2C (Business to Consumer) purchaser – is bombarded with hundreds of messages every day on the radio, TV, the internet, in the newspaper and by a multitude of flyers and advertisements which we often refer to as junk mail.

The messages are all asking the consumer to try this service or this product, and most people have turned off their receptors. It takes uniqueness and originality to catch and retain their attention for even a short time.

Today's Consumer is much more informed about the hit and run type scams and high-pressure tactics that are often used to obtain sales. It is unfortunate that these bottom feeders still exist and will still use these unethical methods for their own financial benefit.

The New B2C Attitude

When today's consumer is faced with a need to look for a product or service; it is often then, that those catchy little ads or jingles, that are stored in the depths of their sub-consciousness, will return to their rescue.

It could also be from a well-positioned ad for that service or product that reaches out to say, "you need me" or "buy me." Despite those possibilities, today's consumer will often simply surf the net to get the latest information on the products or services they want. They will also ask their friends and connections on social media.

They will probably check the sources of those catchy slogans and jingles as well, with a feeling of visiting an old friend.

These slogans and jingles will often have a significant influence on their choice as they are part of the branding process – which is invaluable in today's economy when seeking both B2B and B2C purchasers alike.

Branding Results

This is where sustained, well-constructed and well-placed marketing and imaging will build that sense of familiarity and confidence.

It will place your company's image, your products and services where they will be discovered and remembered by today's purchaser.

Today's social media is perhaps the hottest way of spreading the word about your product or service. It is here that you can engage in an informal way to tell others about your products or service; and have them continue the process, by sharing and liking your posts.

By using these available resources, you can build a strong customer base and stay in touch. Any business that does not take part in social media marketing is missing a large part of their reach potential.

Marketing should not only be used to find new customers but also to keep existing ones. Marketing should include continuous researching of trends and shifts in customers perceived needs and wants.

In this day of quick changing technology not only are products and services changing, but the methods of reaching the marketplace and attracting potential purchases is also changing and evolving.

Marketing Creates Stability

Many businesses will postpone or pass the marketing responsibility on to the sales people (if they have them) and the owners will ignore the marketing part altogether.

They expect the sales person to get out and sell with little or no company participation. It becomes the sole efforts of the sales person to make the company, their products or services visible in the marketplace.

This is not a good policy and will often create hardship and even failure of their sales department; and in the end, their company's demise as well.

Part of Sales Responsibilities

Because this attitude is still very much present, many salespeople have developed marketing techniques to enhance their sales efforts out of necessity; and it is called - Prospecting.

Many forms of prospecting are more marketing than selling functions, and the sales person plays a dual role under the single title of sales. Without company participation, however, the salesperson will find their job to be very difficult to achieve the goals the company may have set for them.

Marketing needs one Captain

If the company's product or service is handled by one sales person who is playing that dual role of sales and marketing, then there is a greater chance of success than if two or more sales people are being used to reach the marketplace with each using different marketing methods.

With each sales person using their own approach, we have the beginning of mixed messages and confusion.

In the absence of a strong marketing plan, brand or vision; what generally will happen, is that this mixed projection of a company's image products and/or services will cause confusion. This will then lead to doubt in the purchaser's mind.

Usually, if the Prospect Doubts it
They will not Buy it

Where several salespeople exist in a company, an owner or sales manager should look after the marketing to prevent this from happening.

Messaging

Marketing requires a clear message, a focused image and identity for each of its products and/or service groups. Successful company marketing through a marketing plan will provide that strong, clear message that will reach many more prospects than would a sales person who is making one-on-one sales calls with their own individual ideas and messages.

A good marketing plan allows the sales person(s) to make the contact with an already informed and interested prospect and do what they are supposed to do – "get the sale."

The Changing Roles

How businesses (the purchaser) obtain information on new and better products for their company has shifted. The purchasers have now assumed the aggressive role in market research.

In Business

The purchaser now searches out the products and services when they are needed to make changes, solve problems, achieve higher profits, or increase productivity or quality.

Connecting with the Purchaser

Many receptionists were long ago replaced with phones in the lobby. The receptionists that remained, became gate keepers.

Buyers are no longer content to wait for help to arrive in the form of a sales person or must scramble through their supply of old business cards.

Even if they were lucky enough to find a card, the sales person has possibly moved on, or the product or service had been dropped from their offerings. Their sourcing information will never be up to date.

GLOSSARY

Advertising Strategy - This will be your outline of your advertising goals, how you will achieve them, and how you will determine the degree of success.

Advertorial - This is advertising that appears to be a news release or editorial in a printed article or publication.

Advertising Research - It is research done to inform you of various aspects of advertising. It could be what methods work best for your products or services, or what consumers are looking for when they view a certain type of advertising.

Affiliate Marketing – This refers to a working arrangement made to market someone else's offerings. The affiliate or sales person will receive payment by the vendor for sales they make.

Branding - This is how you will set your company, product or service apart from the others to achieve their own unique identity or trademark.

It could be a symbol, a logo, a feature, or design that is presented to show company reputation, customer satisfaction, or value. It allows a company to create loyalty for their group of products or services.

Personal Branding - This is the creation of an image or symbol around one's own name that demonstrates the individual's skills, personality, knowledge and integrity and causes people to want to use their services or products.

Brand Perception - Refers to the way the customer will see you, your company, product or service.

Brand Strategy – is how you will demonstrate or present your method of branding to the customer and how you intend to achieve the results you desire and determine they have been met within a timeline.

Brand Vision - This is what you see your branding will achieve for your company in the marketplace. It is the guiding light.

Business Summary - This is a report on your company's history. When it started, who started it and what products and services it started with? This is followed by a history of its journey until where your business is at present day.

This will then generate a description of your existing target market, customer profiles, your products and/or services, their perceived benefits, your competition and their offerings, the advertising vehicles you are using, and what Branding you are using - present day.

Copyright - This right provides the originator of materials with protection from the use of their material by others, by any means, without the originators express consent or acknowledgment to allow that person to do so.

Creative Strategy - This is the structure or outline that determines the nature of the message, the intended recipient, and the message to be delivered. It is also an identifying mark for the way in which copyright protection can be controlled by strategy conformation.

Creative's - This is a marketing term that is used to describe material developed and utilized to generate leads and sales for a company.

DAGMAR - A procedure where goals for an ad campaign are created with a verification process that confirms goals have been met.

Defining **A**dvertising **G**oals for **M**easured **A**dvertising **R**esults

Demographics - This refers to the basic criteria used to classify consumers: location, income, marital status, sex, age, education.

Direct Marketing - This refers to the method by which promotional materials are addressed and sent directly to a person or company by postal services, private delivery or email; rather than by mass media where no company or person is identified as the recipient.

Executive Summary - This term is the same as Business Summary and either term is often used for the same purpose.

Exposure - This refers to consumers or prospects that have seen or heard a message through a media vehicle and it does not matter if they paid attention to it or not.

Focus Group - This is a research method of assembling a small group of people where a qualified interviewer will discuss a product, service or advertising method.

Goals - This refers to a position or level that a company wishes to achieve, the destination for its objectives.

Growth Market - Where you see an expanding need for your products or services.

Holding Power - This means the ability of an advertising vehicle to hold its audience long enough for them to get the benefit of the intended message.

Image advertising - This is how the image of a product or service and its perceived value is promoted.

Implementation Strategy - This refers to how you envision accomplishing your plans, how you will put your objectives into effect and how you will know that you have achieved the intended results.

Infomercial - This refers to an advertisement or commercial that appears to be a news broadcast or talk show, rather than an advertisement of the product or service. It is usually informative in nature.

Integrated Marketing (IM) - This type of advertising refers to the process whereby all aspects of a marketing plan are designed to work together as opposed to working independently.

Keeper - This refers to an item that the consumer will obtain by responding to a promotion or survey.

Loss Leader - This refers to a product or service that has been advertised at an unusually low price to attract prospects or consumers; who the seller hopes will in turn purchase other higher profitable items while purchasing the loss leader.

Macro Marketing - This refers to the ability of a company to adapt to market conditions that are beyond their control for both external and international forces.

Market - It is the place where one sells their offerings.

Market Position - It is the place or position one occupies in the minds of their suppliers, prospects, customers and competition; when reviewing goods and services offered by them as the seller.

Market Profile - This refers to a list of factors such as economic conditions, purchaser types, and competition that relate to a certain market in an area.

Market Research - This refers to the search, documentation and analysis of information relating to the goods or services offered by the supplier and the consumer type in each market and its geographic location.

Market Plan - Establishing products, packaging, services and prices for a target market in a geographical area, to facilitate marketing activities.

Market Strategy - Refers to your plan of attack to put your Market plan into effect and achieve the results you desire.

Market Mix - These are the elements that affect sales such as: pricing, packaging, product benefits and features, distribution methods, and merchandizing.

Market Summary – This refers to your new position after reviewing your existing position and profile, doing your market research and planning.

Marketing – It is the method(s) of approaching, contacting and keeping prospects when you wish them to purchase your offerings.

Marketing Position - This refers to the place you occupy in the minds of your prospects, customers and competition and how they see the success of your marketing activities, such as advertising, branding and the market share you enjoy.

Marketing Profile - This is a list of factors such as economic conditions, purchaser types, competition, and advertising methods used, that relate to a certain market in an area.

Marketing Research - This is researching the marketing activities being used, and to be used, in the advertising or promotion of one's products or services; to enable that they will effectively reach their target market.

Marketing Strategy - It is the way in which you envision the advertising and promotion of your offerings will achieve the company's desired position in the marketplace, and how you will determine your success.

Marketing Summary - This refers to a description of your new position after completing a detailed research analysis of yourself or company, your competition, your markets, the various marketing vehicles, and Branding.

Marketing Mix – It is all the elements that affect sales - often called the Seven P's

> Products (and services)
>
> Pricing
>
> Place (geographical location)
>
> Promotion (advertising vehicles)
>
> People (customers, prospects and employees)
>
> Process (claimed benefits or features)
>
> Physical evidence

MARKETING PLAN - Is the finalized product or plan that you will establish for implementation, to reach your new goals and visions, after doing all your research and creating your marketing summary.

Messaging - It is the presentation of an idea that best tells why the client should buy your product.

Mission – This refers specifically to the process, objectives or steps a company will take to achieve its vision for the future. It outlines how the vision will be achieved. - Its undertakings.

Norms - This represents the behavioral patterns of a group that shows their normally expected reactions and ideals.

Objectives - They refer to the steps or methods a company intends to take so that it can reach its vision or goals. They are the required undertakings to achieve a desired result by a specific time as part of a company's mission.

Offerings - Refers to a total list of products and services that your company has available to offer for sale in the marketplace.

Orientation - The position or direction that an effort or undertaking is focused in.

Orientation Types

Customer Orientated- is where attention is focused on the individual prospect or customer

Product Orientated - is where attention is focused on a product's benefits or features

Service Oriented - is where attention is focused on a service's benefits or features

Market Oriented - is where attention is focused on the intended group of customers or prospects, the geographical area and your offerings

Sales Oriented - is where the company is focused on its sales methods and results

The Four P's - <u>P</u>roduct, <u>P</u>romotion, <u>P</u>rice and <u>P</u>lace

The Five P's - <u>P</u>roduct, <u>P</u>romotion, <u>P</u>rice, <u>P</u>lace, and <u>P</u>eople

The Seven P's - refers to <u>P</u>roduct, <u>P</u>romotion, <u>P</u>rice, <u>P</u>lace, <u>P</u>eople, <u>P</u>rocess, and <u>P</u>hysical evidence

The Law of Triviology – is when people waste more time on small unimportant things that they know and spend less time on larger more complicated and important projects that have a greater effect on their degree of success and a positive financial outcome.

Patronage factor - This represents the reasons for individuals to repeat their purchasing from a supplier or outlet.

Pod casting - is an audio or video file that is presented over the internet.

Positioning - refers to the act of placing your company product or service where you feel it will achieve the most favorable viewing, acceptance, and consideration from your prospects and customers.

Positioning Strategy - refers to the method used or the way in which one feels they will achieve their positioning goal.

Positioning Strategy Types

Defensive Strategy - This occurs if you are a leader and wish to maintain your position.

Offensive Strategy - This occurs if you are not the leader and wish to move up or become the leader.

Flanking Strategy - This will employ focusing on an unchallenged area, using the element of surprise and carrying out a relentless pursuit to achieve dominance.

Guerrilla Strategy - This is where you want more control of a niche. You remain focused and flexible and use hit and run tactics to take over the competitor's position.

Product Position - This is how a product is perceived when compared to a competitor's product.

Product or Service Range - This represents the normal distance a prospect or consumer will travel to obtain a product or service.

Reach - Refers to the number of potential prospects or consumers that a broadcast or advertisement will reach during a designated time.

Research - This is the work done to obtain information required to be able to undertake a certain task. It provides data that can be studied.

It is a search made to compile necessary information to plan your approaches or strategies.

Types of Research:

Conclusive Research - It is research to obtain a conclusion.

Descriptive Research - This means research to answer, "what is".

Desk or internal Research - This is research done from an office or inside location which includes reading articles, magazines, books or researching on the internet.

Exploratory Research - This means investigating an assumption.

Focus Group – It is research comprised of a small group of consumers who are interviewed professionally.

Market Research - refers to the search, documentation and analysis of information relating to the goods or services offered by the supplier to the consumer in each market.

It is research into clientele, geographical area and customer needs and wants to determine if the products and services you wish to provide are right.

Marketing Research - refers to the researching of the marketing activities used in the advertising or promotion of one's products or services, including the research into the various vehicles used to market one's products or services.

In addition to market research; it includes branding and the best ways of implementing the various vehicles used to market or advertise your offerings, to obtain and keep customers.

Predictive Research - It is research to determine future occurrences.

Primary or Field Research - It is research done out in the marketplace.

Qualitative research - It is a method that will determine how a consumer's perceptions and attitudes will determine how they view the attributes of quality.

Quantitive Research - It is a method that measures the number of incidences of consumer trends within a population.

Surveys - It is research done using the telephone, door-to-door, shopping malls, email and postal service for collection of information.

Questionnaire - It is a form that is provided with questions to answer.

SWOT Analysis - This refers to the analyzing of a company's - Strengths, Weaknesses, Opportunities, and the Threats that exist.

Target Market Research – It is research about your intended group of prospects you will approach, to find out if they need or want your product or service.

Vehicle - This refers to a publication or media source that will carry an advertising message to its target market.

Vision - This term represents a company's underlying goals for the future. It demonstrates their intentions or desires for their company, product or services.

The vision is usually achieved by acting out the company's mission. It is a guiding theme for the future.

"End of Glossary"

More on Research

In our glossary, we show many research types. We will deal with just a few of these types in more detail, that could be considered as appropriate methods for what best suits the general needs for a Marketing Plan.

Desk or Internal Research

It is research done from an office or inside location which includes reading articles, magazines, newspapers, books or researching on the internet.

Perhaps the internet will be you're most productive and "time effective" way to obtain the most up-to-date information on the topic(s) of your research.

Files can usually be copied or down loaded making this and excellent way to collect existing data.

If you are part of any social networking groups, this can be an excellent way to gather more information as well as opinions on topics relevant to your research.

This method will usually result in the latest thinking and trends in the marketplace.

Kindle and Amazon

Here you will find a huge source on just about any topic you can think of. Books are usually available in an economical eBook format. For who still prefer a physical item, they are usually available in soft or hard cover formats.

Local Library

One alternative to the office to do this type of research would be at your local library where current and past publications are available, and many books would also be available for one's use. These services are usually free if you are a member.

Book Stores

Your local book store will also have a section that will relate to your search needs, but this will require some sort of investment. You will usually have a choice of ordering in eBook format as well.

It could be considered an investment, if you intend to build a library on what you are researching. In today's changing world your research will require an aggressive continuous updating to keep up with the latest trends.

Primary or Field Research

This is research done out in the marketplace. This field research can easily be done with an existing customer base often through sales and service representatives already calling on these people.

Telephone Research - Existing Customers

You could personally call existing customers by phone, and then visit them for their further input on certain areas that are important to them. For sales purposes this is perhaps the best way to build a relationship.

Next Best - The initial calls could also be made by someone else in the office who is well qualified, for follow up by the sales person on the road.

This research not only provides information that is relevant to your customer base, but it will also build good relations with your customers who will see that you are interested in their ideas and thoughts.

It will show good intentions and your desire to provide a better product or service, and most of all it builds their loyalty.

Telephone Cold Calling Research

To research unknown prospects by telephone becomes a little more difficult, as telephone canvassing is not always received well by the person targeted who is a stranger.

A lot of companies or consumers can be contacted in a day by phone, which makes this method capable of targeting a greater audience.

At 50 to 60 calls easily made in a day, one person can contact as many as 300 consumers in a week and more. It also reduces the high cost for travel and gas as well as time spent to reach your research group.

Your actual participation and feedback results might only be around 10% - 15%. Proper scripting and a well-rehearsed deliverance will provide greater results in terms of feedback.

Clarify immediately that you are making research calls and they are not sales calls.

There are also many research companies who will provide these services to you at a cost. If you do not have the available time or personnel, this could be a good alternative.

Cold Calling in the Field

This is not a time effective way to research unless your products or services are needed by a large majority of people you will be contacting.

The more specialized the offering, the less effective will be your results. You are also faced with the difficult task of getting past the gate keeper.

Questionnaire - This method requires composition of a form that will be provided with questions for the recipient to answer.

This form can be mailed via the post office, emailed, delivered by sales and service people or handled by a professional agency.

If not handled in person, the feedback is slow or non-existent as people hate filling out forms. Being able to provide answers using multiple choice will increase results.

ADVERTISING VEHICLES

An advertising vehicle is the method of advertising used to reach your target market. It is the format used to convey a message from the seller to its intended recipient or the potential purchaser.

This area has almost unlimited scope. One should have a good overall handle on the various forms of advertising that are available to them.

In this section, we will provide a brief description of different vehicles available for your consideration.

NOTE: These descriptions are not intended to provide all the knowledge, or the skills required to use them. We wish only to make you aware of each and encourage you to do further research.

You will need to do your own research and each vehicle type must be fully explored and decisions made as to which direction you will ultimately take to promote your offerings.

Websites

Purpose of a Website

This should be your home base and your social networking base. It should become your business hub. If you do not have a website, it would be a good idea to explore the costs and seriously consider getting one.

The lack of a website is listed by financial lenders as a main contributing factor to business failure. A website brings credibility and shows that you are part of mainstream business activities.

Building your Website

Prices are reasonable if you do it yourself.

There are many "user friendly" web site building programs that are offered by the hosting services, if you want a do-it-yourself method.

If you have no previous web site building experience, it can become a little overwhelming. Determination and perseverance will be your best tools for success.

Done by Others

You can also find web building services to build your site for you. They can range from very basic getting started to advanced and professional.

One danger that exists in going too professional immediately is that you might not know or can properly explain what you wish to achieve. This will probably result in you changing your mind about the site appearance and content after you get used to seeing it or operating it.

Going expensive right away could lead to costly changes, especially if you need someone else to make them. It is best to obtain some basic site management skills to keep your costs down.

If you decide to have someone build it for you, compare three of four sources and do the research. Provide them with examples of sites that you like. Show your design preferences and get quotations with a full description of what you will get.

Ask your peers for referrals

Bringing Traffic to your Site

Many people make the mistake of thinking "build it and they will come" and so they sit with their new website and nothing happens. Learn the fundamentals of attracting prospects.

Placing your website address on your business cards and promotional materials provides credibility and brings some traffic - and it is a start.

Having a site is only the first step; but, it is the door opener for increasing your exposure and your business. You can make use of the many tools that are available to increase awareness and reach new markets.

Free Traffic Methods for Websites

Search Engine Optimization - SEO

This is one step that will increase traffic because the higher your visibility, the more traffic you will attract. You will find many services such as Word Press that will have free SEO building plug-ins such as **Yoast** to help you. (A plug-in is a downloadable tool you can use)

Once you start using SEO, you will become involved in Key words, Title tags, Hash tags, Description tags, Content rules. Navigation, Site maps and other tools for SEO ranking.

There are numerous free sources to help and of course many SEO services with costs. One area to check is YouTube. Just click in SEO methods and review the free tutorials on the subject.

Do your Research First

Try the Free methods first before spending any money here. If you start spending you should start small and find which works best for you, before you spend the large sums that are very easy to do.

Blogging

Blogs provide commentary on a subject. Some will function as more personal online diaries, while others function more as online brand advertising of an individual or company and its products and services.

A typical blog may combine text, images, and links to other blogs, web pages, and another media related to its topic. The ability of readers to leave comments in an interactive format is a very important part of many blogs.

Blogs normally are in reverse chronological order with the most recent blog appearing first on your page or list.

The blogger can choose the number of blogs or the percentage of a blog currently on display with a "read more" option. One may have an archive list of older blogs for people to view and choose for reading.

Blog Types

The personal blog is an ongoing diary or commentary by an individual. Past blogs will also attract traffic with keywords relating to your topic or business.

Corporate blogs are Blogs used to enhance the communication and culture within a company. They can also express thoughts and images externally for marketing, branding or public relations purposes.

Niche blogging is the act of creating a blog to market products or services to a niche market.

YouTube - Video

You can make your own personalized short videos of 1 ½ to 10 minutes by using your own camcorder or webcam and up load your video on YouTube. Use the link provided and place it on your web site, in emails and social medial (where permitted). You Tube *"how to directions"* are excellent.

Many social media websites have maximum time limits ranging from 30 seconds to 15 minutes. Unless your video is very good and has a high level of holding power, keep it at around 3 minutes - 5 minutes max.

It is better for on-line effectiveness to have several short videos for viewers to choose from rather than one long one. Do your research by viewing videos from your niche to see how it is done?

Audio, CD/MP3

For longer more informative narrations it is best to consider an audio CD or MP3 which has a much larger venue for its audience.

They can be played almost anywhere you have a CD or MP3 outlet, in a car, in the home, in your office or anywhere with portable players.

News Page on your web site

Often as a separate page on your web site, you can have a News page that will display recent events in your company or industry. You can archive the past events if you wish.

It is also a good place to show your most recent newsletters in this section even if you send them by email or postal services. This often will bring people back to your site to read your past newsletters especially if they are informative and helpful.

A "Coming Soon" Page

This page on your web site can list upcoming events in your company or your Industry. By including events in your Industry, you can become a go-to-place for what is happening.

Social Media Networking

A social network can be made up of individuals (or organizations) or businesses which are connected by one or more specific types of common interests.

They have common elements such as hobbies, likes, dislikes, friends, financial, business interests, profession, knowledge or entertainment.

It's Origin

The concept of the term "social network" has been used in general for over 100 years to indicate relationships between members of localized social groups and to connect national and international groups as well.

J. A. Barnes started using the term in 1954 to indicate common groupings of individuals by concepts or traditions.

A social network's usefulness to its participants can be measured by its activity, size or operator friendliness.

The Uses

It is common to find that smaller, tighter networks can be less useful to their members for developing their business than networks with lots of open connections and are broader in scope.

Closed networks with many of the same ties and interests offer less fresh input and opportunities to expand or find new potential. A group of friends will be doing things with each other already and will already share the same knowledge and opportunities.

Open networks, with many loose ties and social connections, open networks are often more likely to attract and provide new ideas and opportunities for their members.

A more open group of people with connections to other social worlds will create access to a wider range of information, happenings and business possibilities.

Social networks have also been used to allow organizations to interact internally with each other, utilizing the many informal connections that link together individual employees of a company.

The example of networking power within a company or an organization will often come from the degree to which an individual within that group is at the center of relationships, more than an actual job title or position itself.

Social networks play a key role

- ✓ In the hiring process
- ✓ In job performance
- ✓ In business success

Networks provide ways for companies to gather information deter competition, reach agreements and even present policies for discussion in other various groups.

Your Choices

There are many hundreds of social networking communities on the internet today. We will list only a few examples of the more commonly used ones at the time of this writing.

Their importance may vary with each individual person, company or organization and one should use these examples as only a base to start from and do the research for what fits your own business environment.

We suggest that you continue to explore the large selection of sites so that you can develop and expand your own social networking possibilities.

Social Media Sites

We will not attempt to outline any detailed information relating to what you can do on any of these sites because they are constantly changing. We will provide a general outline of what their role is today.

The best way is to start by searching any new-to-your sites and learning what their current functions are and how you can use them in your business.

Selection

Find the sites that contain your interests and form a common element in your business. When you join them, be an observer at first to get an idea of what is going on.

Learn the terms and conditions of use so you do not get banned by plunging in and breaking the rules. Once you know how they work, participate in them as often as you can.

One main rule of networking is critical. You must reciprocate by providing information to others in the same degree in which you wish to benefit from their information.

Some Social Website Examples

We suggest starting with the free promotional side of these social sites first and learn how they operate before venturing into their paid advertising side.

FACEBOOK - is not only a free personal social networking site, but it also allows one to provide free pages for business outlets to promote their business.

Facebook's paid advertising capability has laser targeted capabilities with 15 plus categories to help you reach your target market with precision.

YOUTUBE - is also a free source for uploading your own videos with a link that will allow you to place the video on your website, emails, blogs and many other marketing locations.

GOOGLE – has almost unlimited recourses to build your business. Some are free as of this writing such as their keyword tool and analytics.

A top SEO ranking on Google will almost guarantee a huge amount of traffic to where it is directed.

LINKEDIN – The use is free and another great site for business professionals and corporate exposure. Their many forums and groups allow one to get exposure and build credibility.

It also allows one to post messages and make business updates that will be seen by their followers.

TWITTER – is also Free and it also allows one to provide a visible personal or business presence.

 Although posts are limited to the amount of characters, there are capabilities of delivering images and more content attached to your posts.

Provide quality posts or you will soon be passed over or eliminated by your intended audience.

REDDIT – is a free source to post material that is voted up or down by its members. There are main categories and sub-categories which will cover most areas of interest. The higher the ranking of an article the more exposure you get.

There are areas where you can also post products or services relating to what you offer.

PINTREST – On this site you create your own areas of interest by finding items and pin them. You can pin something and save it on your board for later or follow it immediately to whoever is offering the product or service.

It's a great place to promote your products or services or find areas of your own interests. There are almost unlimited opportunities to find your own niche social media site to develop your business.

Summary Social Websites

Some of the ways that you can utilize these websites is to optimize their lead sourcing avenues to improve your business exposure and improve and build your client relationships.

It is important that you combine these social networking sites to work with your own website to gain personal and/or business recognition.

Use the individual social sites for their intended purpose and if it is strictly social, use your profile; if you can, to contain links and ping-backs that will send people back to your website or other landing pages.

The Quality links back to your site will build your SEO rankings

And provide more credibility and Traffic.

Research these social sites to find out the best ones to build traffic to your sire and inform your target market of your offerings.

Paid Traffic for Websites

Most of the social media sites will offer some form of advertising capabilities. Learn the ropes and proceed with paid advertising carefully to make sure you are hitting your intended demographics (target market).

Test the results and make sure your ROI - Return on Investment makes sense before going big.

SEO – Search Engine Optimization

Once you have become familiar with the way SEO works you may consider upgrading to a higher level; which is usually at a cost per month or year. With these upgraded versions, you will be able to expand your reach and obtain better results.

Cost per Action - CPA

To bring additional visitors to your site there are methods that will ensure visitors at a cost for the services. If your offerings are in demand and your business suits this type of advertising, it is a sure way to bring people to your site.

The actual selling is still up to you

There are many services ranging from fractions of a penny per action to dollars per visit. Do your research, before you jump in as you can waste a lot of dollars learning the ropes.

Make sure the ROI Return on Investment is enough to justify the expense.

Types of CPA

Pay Per View – (PPV) is usually the lowest in cost as it provides more exposure - but without the guarantee of an actual visit to your site included in your cost.

Depending on your circumstances such as ad quality or your type of offerings; this can often become the more successful method, even without the visit guarantee.

Pay Per Click or Cost Per Click – (PPC or CPC) – In this situation you only pay if the person clicks on your ad and goes to your landing page. That is why this is usually higher in cost as you pay for action taken.

You can become very focused on your prospect choice. After the click the rest is still up to your ad attraction and offerings to complete the next part of the selling process.

CPA is where there are many ways to utilize the traffic to your advantage with specific landing pages where you can collect email addresses for future contact and promotions.

Some CPA Statistics

Often as much as 95% to 98% of people who click do not act at that time. If you do not collect addresses before the client views the actual offer they will usually be lost. Rule of thumb purchasing of good offers is 1% to 2% of the visitors. For good offers it can be much higher.

Using PPA (Pay per Action) to bring interested parties to a landing page where they provide an email address to get free information or move on to the intended source of information, is also very good.

Autoresponders

There are numerous sources (autoresponders) to handle the collection, retention and automated reply to your email lists. Most have very reasonable rates. Monthly costs will usually depend on the size of your lists.

Some Auto Responders Examples

- o AWeber
- o Get Response
- o Mail Chimp
- o Infusionsoft

Control of your Lists

Lists may be segmented to suit customer type or area. You can use any grouping for your lists that you may choose. You can create immediate responses with information, pre-scheduled emails or selected special one-time mailings.

Email is very cost effective especially if it is done by you. Once you have the qualified lists, you can repeat your mailings on a regular basis with the same or different products, services, information and offers.

Internet Broadcasts

A Webcast is a media presentation over the Internet to distribute a single content source of information to many simultaneous listeners/viewers. A webcast may either be distributed live or on demand. Essentially, webcasting is "broadcasting" over the Internet.

Podcasts - replaced webcast in common use with the success of the iPod and its role in the rising popularity and innovation of web feeds.

Phone Casting - means the listening to live or recorded podcasts with a phone. Podcast audiences simply dial up the podcast number to tune in or listen on demand from their phone.

Webinars -The term webinar is short for Web-based Seminar.

It can be a presentation, lecture, workshop or seminar that is transmitted over the Web aimed at anyone who signs up to receive the transmission. In most cases, they are presented with audio availability on your computer speakers.

In some cases, the presenter may speak over a standard telephone line, while pointing out information being presented onscreen, and the audience can respond over their own telephones, speaker phones or by email allowing the greatest comfort and convenience.

It is one of the most common methods being used now to attract clients in larger groups and promote one's ideas or offerings. Webinars are often recorded and can be used over and over to promote one's offerings.

Important to Consider

Do your research for these methods for getting traffic, so that you can optimize the degree of success in your results. A lot of money has been wasted on insufficient knowledge and jumping in too soon.

- Start slow and test the waters first each time.
- Most important factor when getting traffic
  o Is your offering Saleable?

If you do not have something that your prospects will want to purchase, - all the traffic in the world will not be successful. Test market before you spend the dollars. **If it works, then Scale up the promotions.**

Some Tools for the Internet

It is important to find tools that will help save time and money. They can increase your reach and will place you into the latest form of communicating with your suppliers, distributors, sales agents and customers and prospects.

There are many other tools that will also make your job easier and more effective. Spend some time or have someone in your office look for additional ways to achieve these types of results.

Google Analytics

With today's technology, it is possible to gather a great amount of information. Make sure that you employ any available metrics to gather data and it will truly enhance your advertising results.

It is now possible to find out how many people are entering and leaving your web site, how long they are staying and where they stay the longest and the shortest.

You are now able to find out who is opening your emails or on-line newsletters. If you are not taking advantage of these resources, then you are losing out on much of the feedback that is available.

The Benefits

Proper metrics will quickly reveal what works. It will show what works best and what is not working at all. In this way, you can phase out advertising that is not working and replace it with better more productive methods. It can provide both savings and more earning power.

Why They Are Important

Many small businesses operate their advertising in a vacuum. They spend money on a variety of advertising vehicles such as brochures, websites, publications, and an assortment of the many other areas without having a means to measure the effectiveness of each method.

If you cannot tie a sales lead or a sale to its source, then you do not know what is working for you and what is not. To maximize your advertising budget, you need to know which tactic is generating leads, so you can allocate funds to these most productive areas.

Maybe it was a referral from an existing customer or business associate that you should be thanking or returning the favor to. The lead may have come from a tiny ad that was working very well; but, because of your inability to obtain feedback, you cancelled it.

Your To-Do List

Set in place a system that clocks, counts and identifies the lead sources and you will save time and wasted money on ineffective advertising. Ask questions and have your employees ask how the new customer heard about your company or offerings.

Google Keyword Tool

Key words are essential tools when creating web pages or blogs. They are the words that people are using to find their areas of interest.

The Google keyword tool will allow you to find key words that will increase your Search Engine Optimization (SEO) capabilities and allow the search engines to better find you.

Skype

Skype is a peer-to-peer software application rather than a client server system that allows users to make individual voice and video calls and chat over the Internet. Calls to other users within the Skype community no matter where they are located are free.

Skype has also become popular for its additional features which include instant messaging, file transfer, and videoconferencing.

Go-To-Meeting

This is designed to allow the desktop view of a host computer to be broadcast to a group of computers connected to the host through the Internet.

It is a common way to hold both local and world-wide webinars or conduct a company meeting where divisions are spread over large areas that make travel to the meeting expensive and time consuming.

For most meetings involving many recipients, they can easily connect with a temporary download link.

Transmissions can be restricted to those authorized to receive them and are protected with high-security encryption and passwords.

By combining a Web-hosted subscription service with software installed on the host computer, transmissions can be passed through highly restrictive firewalls.

Autoresponders

We have already mentioned this tool earlier, but it is worth mentioning again because of their ability to keep you in touch with your email list on an automated basis

Web Site Plugins

If you are using WordPress to build your site, you should investigate the large choice of plugin tools that will help you enhance your website activity.

Traditional Generated Leads

Free Traditional Methods

Peer Networking

One of the best ways for getting good sales leads is by establishing contact with non-competing owners, managers, sales reps and employees of other companies who are targeting the same demographics as you.

Encourage your sales and service people to talk to their peers in other non-competing companies, who are calling on the same customer types and create some type of reward system for these leads. Keep it simple.

Being introduced by someone that the prospect is already using, and respects is one of the most powerful leads and introductions that you can get.

This takes time to develop and is not a major way when one is first starting out, unless they already have friends and contacts in the industry.

Start building your own network as soon as you can and keep building.

Note: This is called "networking", so always be prepared to do the same in return for your source. This method will soon dry up if you do not contribute or give back.

During the best years of my sales career, 80% of my leads and sources for sales came from peer networking. During my career, peer networking results represented over $ 17,000,000.00 of my annual sales volume for a few years.

Telephone canvassing to selected people

This method is being affected by the growing numbers of gate keepers and no solicitation lists.

In today's business environment, many potential prospects do not want to be disturbed, unless they have made the first contact and thus the role of the gatekeeper has solidified.

Make the calls yourself to ensure effectiveness or designate someone who is enthusiastic and speaks clearly to do the calling for you and provide a list to you of their results.

Highly important is to know the job description of the person who most often looks after the product or service that you are offering.

Your approach may be more affective if you call and get a name first without asking to get through to speak to that person. Some businesses may not provide one and you may need to get a name by other means.

More important – get a name!

Using a name will often get you past the gate keeper. Make sure you have a good presentation. The rule of numbers will take care of the rest. For some products or services, it is still the more cost-effective way to do one's marketing.

Email advertising

Emailing is one of the more cost-effective means of advertising or prospecting, if you have an accurate email list of people or companies that could be interested in your products or services.

A current list of contact names and email addresses, specific to your target market, may initially be hard to secure. Bulk sources for sale are most often unreliable or outdated and no bargain at any price.

Email addresses are not often found on many traditional contact lists making it difficult to build your own using this method.

Acquiring good email contacts is something that you can build upon from your own efforts in many ways such as asking visitors arriving on your site to request free newsletters or other information when they supply a valid email address.

Using Other Peoples email lists

Often it is possible to co-operate with others who are targeting the same demographics but with totally different offerings. They will send a promotion of your offerings to their list and you will do the same for them.

If done properly this can be a trade off without cost especially if the lists are close in numbers.

Cold calling when in the area

When you or your sales representatives are making pre-arranged field sales or service calls, often circumstances will create extra time. Always carry or have your sales/service people carry plenty of promotional material to leave with new potential clients in the area.

Here you will just leave materials and get a name for future use.

Referrals from satisfied customers

Ask for referrals. Have your sales people, your service people and your order desk people ask for referrals. Referrals will materialize unsolicited; but asking for them, will create greater results.

News letters

a) **To Past Contacts** - where no sale was made but there is potential

A method that often works well is sending a monthly newsletter by the postal services directly to your past contacts that did not purchase. This becomes an excellent way of keeping a presence without making continuous follow up phone calls.

Prospects do not feel threatened by newsletters, because they can choose to read them or ignore them, and, they know that usually, you will be none the wiser.

No follow up should be made

Or they will lose their effectiveness

b) **News letters to existing customers**

Existing customers can be great references and can become prospects for new business.

Your company has gained their trust and respect, or they would not be customers, and it is a known fact that often the best sales prospecting is mining your own satisfied customers.

Newsletters give you the opportunity to inform customers of important events in your company, or the industry. Become a source of news, and you will keep your customers, and they will talk about you to others.

Trade Shows – as a Visitor

Often overlooked is attending trade shows as a visitor. Bring lots of promotional material and leave it with people who could be a potential prospect. Make sure you do not interrupt their efforts as a participant and leave if a potential client enters their booth.

Paid Traditional Media

In the following areas, we suggest that not only do you research and obtain the advertising costs but find out the advertising strategies of each method of advertising as described by that source.

What are the benefits for each of these methods and why and how do these advertising sources feel their advertising methods might work for your purpose?

Ask for a list of these benefits that will apply specifically to your business when they provide their quotations.

If they try to just supply you with a standard rate card or advertising portfolio, ask for a separate breakdown in writing explaining how these advertising benefits might apply to your business.

If they cannot do this for you, they are either the wrong source, or it's the wrong vehicle or you need to talk to someone else in the company.

Many media suppliers mistakenly think the rate card or portfolio is all the information that they need to provide you with, and they are very wrong. These things are only sales aids and general outlines of their services.

Ask for specifics.

TV and Radio

Make a list of all the Local TV and Radio stations that cover the geographical area that you are servicing or wish to service.

Call each one and ask for their advertising portfolio for small business. Find out what support they have and how they would put a professional ad campaign together for you.

What choice do you have in quantity discounts? Most will have a plan to suit almost any advertising budget.

Even if you do not feel this is something you will ever do, get the information anyway, because you never know what the future may hold.

Knowledge provides strength and confidence in choosing

Newspapers

Call your local newspaper(s) and get their rates.

Most newspapers belong to a larger group where you can place one ad and get coverage in selected newspapers in other geographical areas outside of your own community, but within your target market.

They too will have discounts based on quantity or frequency of ads and number of locations advertised in.

Billboards

Look for "advertise here" on billboards in your target area and call as many different sources as you can for their rates.

Do not just look at the large ones in fields, look at benches bus stops any stationary location for outdoor advertising.

There will be rates associated with longevity, number of billboards or locations involved. Remember that LOCATION is critical for these ads to be effective.

Be aware that their effectiveness diminishes with time

As they tend to become part of the background

Continuous changing of locations can be good.

Mobile Cards

If you are in a larger community where they have buses or taxis, you may find they also may have what is termed card rates for advertising on their vehicle(s). Find out what they are.

By now you may be saying: "Why do I need to bother with all this stuff as I have never used this type of advertising before, and probably never will"?

We would reply: "If you do not know what these costs and benefits are, there will never be a place for them in your advertising budget.

This information will provide the strongest reason to say no if you feel that you have better and more effective ways to spend your advertising dollar. That decision will be based on knowledge not assumptions.

Socializing (networking)

There is another form of networking that many people use to obtain clients. It is referred to as socializing. It is usually after hours or over weekends.

Some people look for different social functions where they may attend, and they can meet potential prospects.

- It could be a club, a dinner, or exhibit.
- It is anywhere you mingle and meet people.
- It could be joining your local chamber of commerce.
- It could mean arranging or sponsoring your own company golf tournament, fishing trip, or a BBQ.

Usually at these events, people tend to relax and let their guard down. They talk about their families, their hobbies and what they do in their spare time. Often friendships are generated and continued in the workplace. Some will become lifelong friendships.

Investigate how much these events will cost, and you could be pleasantly surprised at how affordable and easy they are to put together.

When sponsoring one of these events, explore ways to create all the beneficial results (leads, branding) for your business that you can.

Trade Shows

As a Participant

A good source of leads can be obtained by being an exhibitor at a trade show. The biggest drawback to this type of advertising or prospecting is that, shows tend to be very expensive.

Experience will reveal ways to save your company from that never-ending stream of extra costs that can quickly accumulate.

Many companies (potential prospects) attend trade shows to secure information for their needs for a process or an upcoming project. They usually send people who will be involved in decision making.

One of the keys to making a trade show successful is to have active and receptive people in your booth. Provide lots of simple but well-designed advertising aids to hand out.

Always have someone standing out front and greeting people in a friendly and enthusiastic way as they go by. This will help demonstrate how well you will service your potential prospect. Take names or get their business cards.

Another asset in being an exhibitor in trade shows is the image-building with potential customers, and the inter-action with your peer group. You become a visible and important part of your industry.

It gives you and your representatives the chance to network from the prestigious level of an exhibitor while developing contacts. Invite your suppliers to help you and build from that side as well.

Become visible as a Visitor

If you are not an exhibitor, attend yourself or designate others to attend. Have them mingle with peers, make customer contact and report their results back to you for follow-up.

Direct Mail to Selected People

Use a good source for current company and employee names. Go through the list and select the type of company, and the level of management you want to contact. If not done by you, have your sales people or office personnel do this.

You can set the parameters of the potential prospect's profile for them to select.

Direct mail is a great method to provide extra prospecting capabilities in off hours. Do a small amount each day and it will hardly be noticed. Once these lists are created they can be used over and over.

Keep the information sent simple and to the point and do not write a short story or a rambling essay. Too many words go directly to the trash.

Less is often more

Having someone follow up asking the person if your information was received, will increase your lead potential. Rely on the rule of numbers, and if you or your sales representative(s) cannot get through after several attempts leave a message, move on and let them call you.

A call that is not returned usually means no interest. A call from them that was prompted by your original letter or a follow up message is a better lead anyway and puts you more in control.

Mass mailing via post office (no stamp)

If your company has a product that is widely used, this method can work well as a third level prospecting method.

Unfortunately, mail without a name and stamp, is often treated as junk and does not reach its intended destination. There is no accountability by anyone involved, and most people know it.

ADVERTISING TIPS

Proper Messaging

Deliver one idea at a time to your audience. Choose the strongest and most positive message available each time you advertise. Select the most compelling reason for your prospect to purchase your products or services and find as many ways to tell the same story that you can.

Select the right style of messaging to suit the vehicle that you have chosen to deliver it, as each type has a different way of presenting your messages.

Continue with the same message until you feel it has reached the greatest portion of your audience and is understood by them. Always make your message clear and deliver it with enthusiasm.

Timing

Many products and their audiences have a time of day, week, month or year that is best suited for presenting the message. It will be when the targeted audience will be most in need, available and receptive.

Give thought if your message can be time delivered in this way - such as on radio or TV. Ask your advertising source what the best time will be for advertising.

It could be time of year sensitive such as chimney cleaning, air conditioning, air make up unit repair. Timing; as they say is everything! It could be advertising pizza when people are driving home or late at night.

Get Attention

Create an ad that has impact and will get their attention. There are many ways to do this with color, sound or a breathtaking view.

Sometimes people will use a jingle or slogan to get attention. Humor and ads with a lot of action are also excellent ways to get attention.

Content

Using good content creates power if it is relevant and of value to its reader. Good Content will leave a stronger impression and keep their attention longer.

It is especially successful in the "social networking media venue" as it will create a ripple effect as an interested reader likes or shares with their followers and their followers do the same and so on.

Promotions

Design compelling offerings that will entice the prospect into purchasing your product or service. It could be a loss leader of some sort which often works well. It should be a necessity.

Loss leaders that are of no real use

Will often Annoy Prospects

If there is nothing tangible offered as a benefit and it does not create excitement and the desire to take advantage of the promotion, it is better not to have done the promotion in the first place.

Fulfill the Need.

It could be a two for one promotion or anything that answers the purchasers question in any promotion, - what's in it for me?

Eighty per cent (80%) of all purchases are based on an emotion which means if you create the right emotional excitement, they will travel to your place of business to obtain the promotion or call to purchase or do so - on line.

Of course, you hope that while they are in their emotional state, they will purchase other products that will provide you with a higher level of profit. This is especially true if they travel to your business location as it helps justify their travel costs.

Inspire Action

It is not enough to just inform your prospects of who you are and what products or services you are offering. You need to cause them to act by appealing to their senses and emotions.

Tell them why they should act now and create the excitement of owning your product or using your service today.

Capturing their hearts with Excitement

Is the doorway to their Wallet!

Honesty and Integrity

Do not attract potential sales with false advertising or misleading advertising. You may get some results, but the word of mouth reaction with an unhappy customer will reach far more ears than your initial advertising.

The negative aspects of misleading advertising have caused the downfall of many businesses. Statistics show that an angry customer talks a great deal more than a satisfied one does.

Be Unique

Be creative in your approach and do something different or unique to get their attention.

In today's busy marketplace it is important to find a way to stand out from the crowd by creating a distinctive informative message that will attract more results for you.

Your uniqueness will make your message stronger and more memorable to its reader, viewer or listener.

As beneficial as it is to be unique, it is very important that you do not appear to be too far from the norm or this will cause people to hesitate before they will place their business with you.

Your ad may be interesting but may not inspire trust. It can be a thin line between greatness and very bad.

Holding Power

After you have obtained the prospects attention you now need to hold that attention long enough to get your total message to them.

A value inspired message offering happiness, comfort, health or prosperity will usually keep the attention span long enough.

The continued use of the same elements that created the attraction in the first place will also help do the job. As the saying goes – Leave them laughing or wanting more. That is the best way to finish an ad.

Retention

Statistics will show that it is 5 times more profitable to spend money on existing customers to get repeat sales additional sales and build continued loyalty.

It is much easier to build on the trust that created this customer in the first place.

Retention can be attained in many ways whether it is with bonus points, or rewards of an unobtrusive manner. You do not want to appear to be buying their business even if that is in fact what you are almost doing. Rewarding their loyalty is good.

The Human Element

It is extremely important to incorporate the human element into your advertising. This will create interaction and relationships with the potential buyer.

People still want to buy from people they trust and like and they will rarely purchase from someone they do not like. Research shows that prospects are more willing to buy from brands that interact with them on a personal and human basis.

This is the reason that social networking is such an effective tool in reaching, attracting and getting people to buy a product or service.

Incorporating the human element and creating interaction is essential. People usually do not buy if the product, brand or advertising has no personality and is difficult to relate to.

Impact of Video Marketing

It has been said that 82% of the US Internet market view videos while on line. Video ads account for over 12% of all videos viewed.

Consumers who watch videos about products are 85% more likely to purchase that product or service than those who do not watch them.

Regardless of the size of your business, a properly designed video is an affordable and very effective tool for advertising.

Publicity

If you can approach a publication with news that will create interest with their readership or even if you have a news worthy item that could be of interest to radio or TV news, they will often provide coverage for free.

Be creative in your approach. Build on it for perhaps a follow up. It's all free publicity and the media loves follow ups.

Choice - Trolleyology

If you own a retail outlet, then investigate the theory of "Trolleyology." It provides information on purchaser's habits.

Most shoppers will look to the right when they are checking out. That is why you will find impulse items lined up on the right side of the checkout Isle or counter.

Have your layout to encourage shopping in a counter clockwise manner as people who shop this way tend to purchase more.

Check out your local grocery store, if they have recently re-arranged their layout you might be surprised to see that the start off direction is counter clockwise.

Orientation

Select your advertising that suits what you are offering and the audience to whom you are offering it.

Certain products will lend themselves to different types of orientation. Some offerings are image oriented while others may be emotionally oriented and so on.

Reach local Audiences

Find sources that will reach your own geographical local markets.

It could be newspapers, or social media, and search engines that are designed to find information in someone's local marketplace.

It is better than using mass market media where most of your audience is too far from your location to be interested or take advantage of your offer.

Search Engine Key Words

Make sure your web site contains the key words that will attract search engines to your products and services. This is very important when setting up your site and when you are updating it to present new offerings.

Positioning

It is the place you occupy in the minds of your prospects or customers when compared to your competition. Many companies use adjectives to position themselves in the minds of prospective customers.

Words like quality, convenient, cutting edge and latest technology when associated with your company, its products or services will set you apart or favorably position the clients trust and confidence.

Often some words or phrases become overused and annoying to the customer so always try to be up to date on what is on the way out.

The in keywords or phrases represent something that they wish to be associated with. Your position or the place they see you occupying, will determine if they will select you for your offerings.

Analytics

There is little point in advertising if you do not know what it is doing for you. Ask the purchaser how they heard about you. Teach your employees, your sales and service people who see the new customer in the field, to ask how the customer heard about you.

To advertise blindly without checking results is like planning a weekend family BBQ without checking the weather forecast. It is like covering your ears when you are getting important advice.

You do not want to continuously send out advertising if it is not working for you.

Successful advertising is never expensive. If you are trying something new that is more than you would usually spend, it is critical to measure the results.

A type of advertising that costs $50.00 and creates 2 sales is more expensive than a $400.00 ad that creates 25 sales for the same product.

MARKETING CONCEPTS AND THEORIES

The four P's = SIVA

1) <u>P</u> is for <u>Product</u> – <u>S</u> is for <u>Solution</u>

> Your product must provide a Solution to the customer's problem.

2) <u>P</u> is for <u>Promotion</u> – <u>I</u> is for <u>Information</u>

> Your promotion must provide enough information to allow the client to make a well-informed decision.

3) <u>P</u> is for <u>Price</u> – <u>V</u> is for <u>Value</u>

> Your price must reflect Value for what they are receiving in return.

4) <u>P</u> is for <u>Place</u> – <u>A</u> is for <u>Accessibility</u>

> Your place must be accessible and convenient to provide products and services.

Step Outside of the Box

It has been said that it's hard to read the label when you are inside the box

It often happens that we become too involved in our own day to day activities and the advertising patterns in our industry to be fresh or different in our creative attempts to advertise.

If you create your own advertising, use your suppliers for advertising tips, and get their ideas as well. If you are already using their ideas and they are not working, look outside the box for different ideas.

It is good to periodically explore new opinions outside of your normal advertising group to avoid continuous use of the bad habits that are often picked up and incorporated into advertising.

Becoming too Complacent

It is easy to become repetitive and boring using the same ideas over and over. Often advertisers do not even pay enough attention to see if their ads are working well for them.

They tend to approach advertising as an inconvenient task that they need to quickly get out of the way, so they can get on with more important things. It is too easy to fall into this trap.

If one is not catching any fish maybe, it's time to change the bait or even the stream or part of the lake that they are fishing in.

Step outside the box, try something different or unique that will get those creative juices and enthusiasm flowing again.

Maybe you will discover a better way to attract your prospects; and advertising might even become an enjoyable task, if it's working.

Word of Mouth

Word of mouth advertising is free, but it can also become your worst enemy if it is not handled properly. Never assume that every customer is saying good things about you all the time. Perhaps your company did not deliver on time or it sent the wrong item.

Yes, you corrected it; but did you follow up the correction with a visit to apologize for your mistake, and pledge to make every effort to not let it happen again. Did you remove the anger or stinger and their urge tell others of your mistake?

We often overlook the reasons why the word of mouth advertising may not be giving us what we think we are getting.

Often these mistakes; that cause negative comments, are quickly covered up internally; and as an owner or manager, you may not even know about them, unless you discover them accidentally.

Social media has caused companies to become more transparent and they must openly address complaints and problems or pay the consequences.

When you respond quickly anywhere; especially online, you can often avert a potentially devastating blow to your reputation. It is best to also implement a review practice by calling your customers or even visiting them on a regular basis if possible.

It is a known fact that unhappy customers talk more about the problems that you have caused than the good things you have done. It is human nature to do this, so make sure the right word of mouth is happening for you.

The other results from "implementing a review process" will be the elimination of the tendency for your employees to cover these things up. It also will build customer loyalty and provide the opportunity to turn a negative occurrence into a positive action.

Six parts to Implementing Brand Strategy

1) Develop a well-defined clear brand identity.

2) Determine what your brand objectives will be and who will be responsible for carrying them out.

3) Concentrate on your intended market or you will hit everything. Spending time on the wrong market is not only a time waster but a money waster.

4) Find and eliminate obstacles to your Branding.

5) Make sure your logo, card, letterhead, advertising and packaging all reflect your branding message and are the same.

6) Write a jingle or slogan that people will remember.

Podcasting and Webinar Tips

- Create Immediate Attention.
- Provide multitask functions or choices - watching, listening or downloading.
- Offer experience and a willingness to share industry information, guidance, or advice.
- Offer benefits.
- Apply to the need for self improvement of mind and body, or the desire to improve one's product quality or solve a problem.
- Deliver a well focused message for each broadcast.
- Choose your point of discussion, select good content to support it and illustrate the message. Keep it short and to the point.
- Make it entertaining and use people language.
- Speak clearly so there is no guessing at words or missing them altogether.

Keep your podcasts/webinars regular and consistent. Follow an organized schedule as opposed to a hap hazard schedule where people will soon lose interest and stop following.

Areas to review in Making Top Videos

- Convert their viewing into your Sale?
- Direct them to your place of business, web site's product or services pages.
- Create an desire to take immediate action to call you or make a visit to your premises or your web site.

Create a script that is professional and has good content and deliver the message professionally and enthusiastically.

- Chose an appropriate dress or wardrobe to suit the occasion and decide how to present it.
- Edit it. If it is a head shot, body shot, inside, outside, home or business or manufacturing atmosphere make the transitions from one area to the next smooth?

What's in the Background?

It is often surprising and sometimes very embarrassing what shows up in a video. Often, they are items that one sees every day and takes for granted. They become part of your unseen background.

Know Where you will Install the Video?

- Is it on your website for viewing, on your website to purchase, or on a social network site for viewing?
- Know how you will track the results?

Integrated Marketing - IM

IM is the key to establishing a clear and defined message that will be delivered to your prospects.

Make sure that each part of your advertising is acting in harmony with all other parts and together they are projecting your overall message and enforcing your branding strategy.

This is a key factor in making sure you are getting the most out of your advertising dollar.

Target Audience

Create a close connection with your target audience by making sure you are talking to the right people.

Example One

You are selling children's clothes or shoes, so ask yourself who is my target market?

The children are the recipients and you must appeal to them visually and emotionally at their level; but the real target market is a dual target market with the main decision maker being the parents or other caring adult.

The advertising must deliver an effective message to them before the messaging is complete or action will not be taken.

Example Two

If you are selling tools to the industrial sector, who is your target market?

It could be singular, but it also could be dual. It might be the person responsible for managing costs like the plant manager, but the tool is being used by someone on the assembly line.

Your promotion needs to appeal to both because success will not come unless you have the support of both parties. Your advertising must be designed to get the attention of both and appeal to both.

Your dual message would show the economic benefit or increased productivity for the manager and the ease of use to the operator.

Advertising Mistakes

Many small businesses do not investigate advertising vehicles well enough, and quickly jump into an ad campaign so they can feel they are doing something to promote new business.

Often, they hate the advertising process and allow non-productive ads to run continuously simply because they have not made the effort to obtain feedback or accountability. Frequently it is just indifference.

Make the sales person promoting your advertising accountable for what they are recommending. Many advertising agents are more intent on the sale or filling space than providing something that is working for you.

Have a Positive Marketing Attitude

Many entrepreneurs have some marketing knowledge but do not have the right marketing attitude.

They may have experienced the result of doing a poorly planned marketing effort in the past and spent a lot of money and nothing happened. No calls came in and no new business resulted

Marketing is often mistakenly seen as a negative side of the business. You must tie it to a positive result like cheques or orders in the mail.

Some people sabotage their situation with excuses. "If I look after my clients, I will get repeat business and referrals so why do I need to have a marketing plan or need to advertise at all."

Another excuse is: "I do not have time for marketing. Marketing is uncomfortable and not what I enjoy doing. It is a waste of my time and company money."

These types of excuses are often the prelude to Failure"

SUMMARY PART ONE

In this Part one of this book, we have provided a base of terms, definitions, concepts and theories which should allow the reader to take the next part which is to create and implement their own marketing plan.

PART 2 –

CREATION AND IMPLEMENTATION

Part Two is divided into Four Sections

S1- Information and Statistics

- Why marketing plans are essential
- What lending institutions consider essential ingredients for a loan?

S2 – Marketing Plan Components

- You will first learn what the basic components of a marketing plan are before you begin the process of creation one

S3 – Marketing Plan Creation

- Once you understand what the different components are; we will provide a step by step process of questions you need to ask, to create your own plan.
- In putting your own marketing plan together, you will find it necessary to look at all the aspects that will make your business successful.

S4 – Plan Implementation

- The final part of the process is taking your plan and showing you how to put it into operation.

Creating a marketing plan will allow the creator to become intimate with the company. Often it will lead to discovering why progress or growth has been slow or non-existent.

It will cause one to review all aspects from the company's beginning right up to present day, and to research new markets and learn about competition.

It Enables the Creator to make their own

"Blueprint for Success"

A Marketing Plan

S1 – INFORMATION AND STATISTICS

Why People Start a Business

People start their own business for many reasons.

1. They want to make more money

2. They want more freedom

3. They want independence, control of their future

4. Their employer is downsizing, and they have been laid off

5. There is a long strike with no end in sight

6. Dissatisfaction surrounding someone's present employment for any reason such as:

    o Shift work,

    o Not enough hours,

    o Too many hours,

    o Too much travel, or

    o Stuck behind a desk

7. A company could go out of business and several splinter groups may be created to start up their own ventures.

In most cases the new business owner can start with a small customer base. Their start could be with a company or several companies that they have serviced for years while working for their previous employer.

They have provided excellent service and developed a good relationship.

The client has become reliant on their skills or business integrity and this initial customer base is often enough to justify starting their own business.

Why is a Marketing Plan Important, if statistics say over 80% of small businesses do not have one?

You need only to look at the number of businesses like yours, doing the same service, or offering the same products and then - look at how many have staying power.

If one looks close enough, they will see that the companies, who remain in business and are profitable, will have some sort of marketing plan.

You may say: *"If I start with a good base of customers and do a good job for them, should that not be enough to keep my business going?"*

The answer could be: *"Yes if you are lucky."*

Why do we say Lucky?

Because of your Macro Environment

Macro Environment

One of the things that will affect your future business will be your Macro Environment.

Your Macro Environment is made up of the external and internal threats to your business that you have no control over. You must adapt to them, if you wish to survive - because you cannot change them.

Sample Macro Environmental Threats

- The Company who supplies most of the work for your business has closed shop and moved to a location too far away for your company to service.
    - Their decision will not be influenced or affected by your loss of their business or your disappointment.
    - It will certainly affect your position and you have no control over it.
- What happens if your key client has a personnel change and your contact of five or ten years retires or leaves for another job?
    - There is now a new person in their place with their own purchasing contacts and favorites and you are now on the outside looking in.

How are you Affected?

If you have been complacent in your approach to obtain new business, you may find yourself immediately scrambling for its replacement. These are only several examples of changes that you cannot control.

These types of events are commonplace in the volatile marketplace of today.

Companies who are your customers, are continuously re-positioning themselves. They too could find themselves downsizing to stay alive or end up closing their own doors.

Why Marketing Plans?

You have managed to get your business going and many of the initial unknown new areas are now under control.

However, there is something deep down inside that is telling you that you should be able to have more control over your destiny and ensure success.

Maybe you are tired of being in a wait and see situation.

You may be asking yourself:

o   What more can I do to ensure success and profitability?

o   How can I find ways to obtain more business and out maneuver my competition?

o   Why am I still struggling just to stay alive?

New businesses usually start with a great deal of optimism, energy, enthusiasm and anticipation of good things ahead.

This is good, and it should be so

As we said earlier, often new companies can bring existing work or clients from their connections with their recent employer's customer base. This will provide their start.

People Dislike Negative Reports

Almost no one wants to look at the overwhelming statistics of what happens to most new businesses starting out. This is especially true in their early days when they have just started themselves.

They feel that they do not need to know these cautionary facts as they are enthusiastic with their new venture and are not yet faced with very many negative challenges.

Unfortunately, statistics will show that the survival rate for new businesses is very low.

Why are these Statistics Important?

They are important because knowing these facts will help prevent the new business owner from making the same mistakes that most new businesses will make. These mistakes are often why they fail.

Statistics are also what banks and other financial institutions base much of their lending practices on.

They must know these statistics to make wise decisions when providing financial assistance to any business whether it is new, growing or seasoned.

Our Research consisted of the following Sources:

11. Industry Canada – Small Business Research and Statistics

12. Government of Canada – Canadian Business Network

13. Government of Canada – Services for Entrepreneurs

14. Research on Small Business report

15. Statistics Canada

16. SBA – Small Business Administration

17. Dun & Bradstreet

18. Chartered Banks

19. Wikipedia

After reviewing the information from the above sources, we then summarized what we found, and we put together the information found on the following pages.

The answers to these three questions are important.

1. What makes a business successful?

2. What causes most businesses to fail?

3. What are the chances of success or failure for any business?

1.A Successful Business has:

- Sound Management Practices
- Good Planning ability
- Good background and Experience in the business
- Products or Services that solve needs
- Good Technical and Service support
- Good business plans, marketing plans and sales plans

2.Failure is Caused by:

- Poor financial skills
- Lack of planning – no business, marketing or sales plan
- Lack of experience and unrealistic expectations
- Insufficient knowledge of competition
  - Their strengths and weaknesses
- Insufficient capital
- Poor management
- Misplaced efforts *(Law of Triviality) *see part 1glossary
- Poor understanding of target markets
- Amount of effort made is insufficient to reach targets
- Poor location
- Low sales
- No website
- Overspending

3.The Chances of Success or Failure

Worldwide there are about 50 million new businesses starting every year. This represents approximately 137,000 per day. On the same basis, there are 120,000 businesses worldwide that terminate operations each day.

A Study by Statistics Canada found the following relationships between Canadian business starts and closures.

> In a year where approximately 144,000 – 145,000 Canadian businesses were starting up; it showed, that during the same time there were about 136,000 to 137,000 businesses closing.

These figures demonstrate why it is important to study what makes businesses succeed as well as what makes them fail.

The wise business owner should be aware of both areas, so they can do what is necessary to avoid closure.

Per a Dunn and Bradstreet Report

Each year out of every 100 businesses with fewer than 20 employees starting in business we find the following results:

- Only 37% have a chance of surviving 4 years
- 20 – 30% have a chance of surviving 5 years
- Only 9% have a chance of surviving over 10 years.
    - Meaning 91% will fail within 10 years of start-up
    - Approximately 10% of those failing go Bankrupt
- Approximately 90% of those closing within 10 years, cease operating because they were not successful.

With these overwhelming odds against success it is no wonder financial institutions look for certain elements in a business before they will consider any kind of assistance.

We also found there was little difference when worldwide figures were compared to the Canadian figures used in this report. Survival is also closely associated with size and age of the firm.

The longer they have been in business and the larger that they have become - the more likely they are to continue in business. Lending institutions look for the main reasons for the success or failure of a business. If it is so important to them, should it not also be important for the small business owner to know as well?

What These Studies Revealed

Most studies conducted to find out what makes a company succeed or fail; stated that one of the main reasons for failure was the lack of a good business plan or marketing plan.

At the same time, they indicated that one of the main reasons for success was having a good business plan and marketing plan. Therefore, one of the first things that any bank or lending institution will ask for when you need assistance, is your business and marketing plans.

When Starting Out

Most people do not do a market study, nor do they take the time to learn many of the skills that will eventually come to play a very important role in operating their own business.

They often do not put together a business plan and if they do, it usually does not include a marketing plan or sales plan.

They may simply deal with the business at hand and set about servicing their newly acquired customers and try to keep overheads as low as possible.

You may say: "Why look at negative things"?

We know that no one starts a business with the intention or thoughts of failure. The obvious determined outlook for most is to think positive and not negative. This is of course the right way to think.

However; this statistical knowledge is important!

One should know the right and positive things to do to make their business successful.

At the same time, they need to become just as aware of the pitfalls and the where, why and how many people lose control of their company.

Since we have just discussed the failure statistics and stated why most businesses fail, it is our intent to show you the framework that is essential for creating

"MARKETING PLANS"
Why?

Implementation of a good marketing plan will put you in the positive outcome zone and avoid becoming a failure statistic yourself.

If banks and financial institutions make such an effort to know what makes a business more likely to succeed than to fail, there must be good reason for this attention.

Do not wait until you are forced to go into crisis management mode to survive. This is never an environment for making good business decisions, being objective or learning new procedures.

Why you should have a Marketing Plan

When one looks at an outline of a business plan it is very evident why Marketing is necessary in the success of a business. At a glance, you have all the components to make your business a success.

In most cases the business plan and marketing plan are spoken in the same breath because they are so closely tied together. So why do so many small businesses ignore or put off what will provide the best opportunity for success?

Perhaps they think that these things are a waste of time and they should be looking after their customers and business at hand.

And YES, they should look after their clients.

But there is more!

A Typical Business Plan Includes parts 1 - 8

1. The Management Team
2. Financial Plan
3. Operations Plan
4. Financial Forecasting
5. Human resources Plan
6. Environmental analysis (where required)
7. Marketing Plan
8. Sales Plan

Marketing Plan Components (Items a - n)

    a. Management Study and Duties

    b. Business Summary

    c. Business Description

    d. Industry Background

    e. Goals and Objectives

    f. Research

    g. Market Summary

    h. Business Strategy

    i. Competitor analysis

    j. Market analysis

    k. Advertising review

    l. Market Strategy

    m. Branding

    n. Implementation of Objectives

Normal Practices for Businesses when Starting Out

Most businesses starting out will handle the items shown in our typical Business Plan in this way.

Item 1 The Management Team will be the owner or owners wearing many hats.

Items 2 to 5 usually do not take any formal shape and the business runs with the start-up capital and sales cash flow.

Item 6 – Environmental Study - occurs only in special circumstances and business type.

Item 7 – The Marketing Plan – (parts a - n) The new business owner may have some types of advertising or brochures made, but usually there is no operating marketing plan. Often marketing is left up to the person responsible for sales.

Item 8 - **Sales Plan** consists only of servicing their existing clients and making a few calls on similar businesses.

General Notes

Statistically; the business person who is best equipped for success, will be one of the 20% that will incorporate a quality marketing plan into their daily operations.

They also develop their own sales plan and selling skills or hire someone qualified in sales to handle the sales leads produced by marketing.

By doing these things, not only are they creating more stability for themselves, but for their employees.

You must approach your business with the idea that you must grow in some degree to stay the same or even survive. You need to allow for the setbacks that often occur and are beyond your control. A good marketing plan will provide this capability.

Marketing Plan Misconceptions

Some small businesses feel that they have a marketing plan, but they only have an advertising method that they use when the need arises. Their marketing, advertising and sales efforts begin after-the-fact.

> This type of reaction time can be costly and create many hardships for a business to recover from. Some do not recover.

> If their advertising or sales efforts eventually bring in prospects and some business, they feel they are OK. They have managed to survive one more time.

In today's changing world of business, marketing methods also change, and many methods quickly become outdated and ineffective.

Small businesses offering a service or related product are often based on the owner's background experience or trade. Often the owners have not been exposed to the world of sales or marketing.

They simply set up shop and service their initial client(s).

Many will start looking for additional work immediately, but some will procrastinate and begin to look when they are in a crisis mode.

Because marketing and sales may be a totally new territory for them, the lack of a strong marketing presence or marketing plan is something that they should be placing high on their essential list of things-to-do.

The Desire to Expand

Initially these new businesses have carried over some residual contacts from their previous employment which provides them with their initial staying power.

Whatever the reason for starting their own business, they will soon be faced with their own growing needs to increase or replace lost sales.

They may be the best at what they do in their trade or service, or they may have the best product; but, how do they get that message out into the marketplace so that consumers or prospects can tune in.

Analogy

Before a farmer can plant their crop and expect it to grow, they must plan which fields they will use. They must then cultivate the soil.

Once they have planted the seed, it does not end there. They must then water and fertilize their fields to ensure a good crop and harvest.

Business is no Different

To expand, the business owner must also operate in the same manner.

They must:

- **Research** (find the right customer demographics)
- **Select** (focus on the target market)
- **Prospect** (find the qualified clients)
- **Cultivate** (find needs)
- **Fertilize** (build trust and desire)
- **Harvest** (get orders)

Marketing - is the researching, selection of the right target markets and attraction of qualified prospects. It is the preparation and planting of the seed to be cultivated by sales.

Sales – Further qualifies and cultivates by establishing needs, building trust and finding solutions. The final part of sales comes with harvesting or obtaining the order.

To successfully achieve the above, one must create and implement a successful marketing plan and have a qualified sales person to complete the task.

S2 – MARKETING PLAN COMPONENTS

Our Marketing plan profile is aimed at businesses where the company has not yet developed a marketing department or plan. In many smaller companies the owner often looks after sales and advertising on a *"when needed bases"*.

For many owners who lack sales or marketing skills; the answer to increase sales, usually results in the hiring of a sales representative. Too often, this person also does the prospecting (which is the extent of the Company's Marketing).

That is why Marketing Plans often do not happen

As companies become larger, these responsibilities often grow apart.

The once singular sales representative position expands into Accounting, Marketing, Sales Managers and more Sales Representatives.

As stated earlier, this book is written primarily for the company where these hats are still worn by a few (one to three individuals); so, it does not make sense for us to try and designate separate responsibilities here.

It will be up to the owner to decide, who wears which hat.

It is also written for the Sales Manager who is actively selling and has one or more sales representatives under his management control.

In the following section, we will be providing explanations of the Eight Main Components of a normal Marketing Plan shown as 1.0 to 8.0

We will also show their sub-components such as extensions of these main components (Such as 1.1 or 1.1.1 and so on).

The Components Explained

1.0 – Business Summary

This is a report on your company's history from start-up to present. Parts of the business summary can be used in the future as:

- An introduction for new employees to learn about your company
- A base for "about us" on your website or to introduce your company to prospective customers
- In your promotional brochures.

Most of all, doing this will cause you to re-visit your roots, re-acquaint yourself with the past and how you have evolved – your good moves and your bad ones as well.

Your Business Summary 1.1 – 1.4

1.1 – The Starting Day Summary - This will be a complete description of how things were when you were starting out.

1.2 - The Journey Summary - This will be a description of everything that happened and changed from your starting day right up to present day.

1.3 - Present Day Summary - This will be a complete description of how things exist present day.

1.4 - Recommendation Summary - Based on review of your history, you will make a list of recommendations what changes or improvements should be considered for the future.

2.0 – Situation Analysis

Your situation analysis will be a further review where you will examine your company and competition using the following profiles.

2.1.0 – Analysis Profiles for Your Company

2.1.1 - S.W.O.T. Analysis - stands for finding your Strengths, Weaknesses, Opportunities and Threats.

2.1.2 - Macro Environment refers to the internal and external forces that you cannot change but must adapt to; whereas, the results of the SWOT analysis are changes that are within your ability to control.

2.1.3 - Products and Services Offerings is a full description of all your products and services.

2.1.4 - Customer Base is a complete breakdown of your existing focus area and customer list. Their demographics

2.1.5 - Geographical Boundaries will have a certain reach, restriction or boundary limitation. Consumers will usually have a geographical radius that they will travel in, to obtain certain products or services.

2.1.6 - Present Market Position: where do you see yourself in the marketplace regarding market share and image as compared to your competition? Are you #1 or #2 or further back in the pack?

2.1.7 – Analysis of Sales and Service - What factors are affecting your sales and sales department?

2.1.8 – Recommendation Summary – You will make a list of recommendations from 2.1.1 to 2.1.7 and of the steps you can take to improve your position over each of them.

You will Review these Recommendations

When you create your Marketing Plan Objectives

2.2.0 – Analysis Profiles for your Competition

2.2.1 – Their S.W.O.T. Analysis - finding their Strengths, Weaknesses, Opportunities and Threats.

2.2.2 – Their Macro Environment - the internal and external forces that you cannot change but must adapt to

2.2.3 – Their Products and Services Offerings - a full description of all their products and services.

2.2.4 – Their Customer Base - a complete breakdown of their existing focus area and their known customer list. Their demographics

2.2.5 – Their Geographical Boundaries – The geographical area that they service

2.2.6 – Their Present Market Position – Where do you see their position in the marketplace?

2.2.7 – Analysis of their Sales and Service efforts – What factors affect their sales efforts?

3.0 – Marketing Strategy

Marketing Strategy: Refers to your plan of attack to reach your marketing goals for all your products or services. Answering the following from 3.1 to 3.8 will help form your marketing strategy.

3.1 - Marketing Vision: This term represents your company's underlying marketing goals for the future. It demonstrates your intentions or desires for your company, products or services.

The vision is usually achieved by acting out the company's mission. It is a guiding theme for the future.

3.2 - Marketing Mission: Your marketing mission will outline how you will achieve the marketing vision, who will do it and when?

3.3 – Marketing Goals: Your goals are what you want your efforts and your marketing plan to achieve by a certain date.

They are the indicators - the beacons that guide you, your company and its marketing to reach your vision and mission statements.

3.4 - Target Markets: that could provide you with the possibility to expand into additional market segments within this same geographical area with your existing products or services or with new offerings or develop new areas. They are made up of 3.4.1 to 3.4.3

> **3.4.1 – Growth markets** - What part of your market is growing and expanding.
>
> Is there a new Residential, Industrial or Commercial development that is bringing new potential?
>
> Are existing customers expanding their production?
>
> **3.4.2 – New Markets** - Are there areas that you have recently discovered that could add to your existing sales? Are there new uses for some of your offerings?
>
> **3.4.3 – New Product development** - New Products or Services that you have created or are available to be developed or added.

- Are there exclusive distribution rights for offerings that no one else has in your area?

3.5 – Marketing Positioning Strategy - Determine what your current share of the market is.

Decide what you need to do to reach your sales goals and what attributes you will give your offerings to achieve them.

- **Defensive** – If you are # 1 and want to remain there

- **Offensive** – If you are not #1 and want to move up

- **Flanking** – If you want to go after an unchallenged area

- **Guerilla** – If you want to take over a competitor's niche

3.6– Advertising Vehicles: Research and decide which advertising vehicles provide the best means to reach your target markets.

3.7 – Marketing Mix - The marketing mix can be determined by the 7 P's. If the positioning statement makes certain claims, the 7 P's must be clearly constructed to demonstrate your claims are true.

1. **Product** – If you say it has superior taste – then it must have it.

   If your product requires Department of labor approval or needs to meet health and safety codes - it must have these attributes.

2. **Price** – If you say your price is affordable – it must be affordable to those who would need your offerings

3. **Place** – If you say you are conveniently located – you must be.

4. **Promotion** – If you say your service is quick - it must be quick. If your promotion says it is easy to operate or will save time, then it must deliver those promises.

5. **People** – If you say your people are friendly - they must all be.

6. **Process** – If you claim your service is reliable – it must be.

7. **Physical Evidence** – If stated your gym is well equipped – it must be.

3.8 – Sales Strategies – Recommendations from your sales and service departments

Marketing Recommendation Summary: Your recommendations are comprised of a list of steps or procedures detailing what you need to do and who will do to create your marketing strategy.

You will Review these Recommendations

When you create your marketing Plan Objectives

4.0 – Branding

Branding is your promise to deliver certain attributes of your offerings on a consistent basis to your customers. It is your guarantee to deliver those benefits and attributes without fail every time.

Branding is conceptual in nature and is your pledge of performance. It is what builds trust and confidence and demonstrates that your product will deliver the benefits that the customer is looking for.

Branding is often called creating a trade name or an identity that is uniquely and distinctly yours and different from the competition.

Many larger companies will even separate their subsidiaries with trade names to keep identification easier, and more definite.

Brand marketing is the way of propelling your business into public view and it becomes invaluable in the struggle to obtain and retain customers.

Your Brand is your Word

Branding is the process of giving your company, product or service a distinct identity. It gives you the name, a trademark. It provides goodwill, creates customer satisfaction and builds loyalty.

Branding creates value and perceived benefits and can become the greatest determining factor for success in your marketing efforts.

Branding will provide an identity for your company, your products and services.

It will provide a focal point and a base from which you can work to create greater loyalty with your existing customers and build confidence in your prospects mind.

Brand Perception

Brand perception is the deeper awareness of the value and benefits that customer has experienced from the use of your offerings.

If people trust a brand they will continue to be loyal customers and recommend your company its products and services to others.

Brand perception can create added value for both functional and emotional needs that demonstrate superior attributes over the competition.

To perfect the image that, you desire, you must do the research that will determine who your target audience will be, and how you want them to perceive your brand and your market position.

4.1 – Brand Identity

Branding gives your company, product or services its own attributes, a personality and enforces expected results. A brand identity becomes reality and exemplifies a feeling of trust, security and confidence.

Product Brand Identity

Branding can create a trade name for your products; but most of all, it will provide an identity separate from that of your competition.

The most important factor is to maintain the quality of the brand name with each new product introduced.

All new and existing products must remain consistent or they all may be affected; especially as seen by those new consumers or companies that are just emerging into the marketplace.

Service Brand Identity

The same conditions apply to the world of services. Services can be a more difficult area to control simply because they may depend on the efforts of many different individuals or outlets.

It is important to have "in-place" a strong branding policy and a good checking process that both the customer and the service persons are aware of. This awareness increases customer confidence and loyalty.

Corporate Brand Identity

Building a corporate identity is more difficult than that of a single product or service because of the complex nature of a business or corporation.

The branding identity must flow through the entire organization from the reception area to the shipping department.

It must be there in the sales department, the accounting process, the estimating department, the engineering, the manufacturing, and be demonstrated in the attributes of your products and services.

All your employees must be aware of your Branding and Corporate identity and must also adhere to those principals outlined in your **4.2 Brand Vision** and **4.3 Brand Mission.**

As soon as you have established your vision and mission

Post them for Everyone to see

Personal Brand Identity

This type of branding can be utilized best by a stand-alone person (not usually a company unless it is their name). It promotes their knowledge, talents, products or services.

Personal branding will promote a person's name and associate that name with the qualities they wish to illustrate in their products or services and endorsements.

The products and services provided become an extension of their personal branding efforts. You see the person or hear their name and you think quality, enjoyment, happiness, body health or whatever their brand identity provides.

4.2 – Brand Vision

It is what you see your branding process will achieve for yourself, your company and in the marketplace. It is the guiding light that will take you to your branding goals and create your successes.

It is a Market Position to be Reached

Or a Customer's Perception to be Achieved

Without establishing a "Brand Vision," you will find it difficult to determine what you want personally, for your company's brand and for your customers.

You will need to create it before establishing the recommendations required to reach your goals and the success you desire.

You will need it before you can create your brand mission and brand strategy, which will encompass the process, objectives or steps that a company needs to take before they can achieve their branding goals.

Brand Vision is necessary and will take form in the brand mission and marketing plan.

4.3 – Brand Mission

Brand mission refers specifically to the process, the recommendations, objectives or steps a company will take to achieve its Brand Vision for the future. It outlines how the vision will be achieved.

The Brand Mission should state in detail the person or group who will be responsible for carrying out this mission, what the steps will be, and a time frame in which it is to be carried out.

4.4 – Branding Goals

Branding goals are the measuring points and the destination points that will allow you to set your course to achieve your Brand Vision.

You will set these goals to be achieved in a certain time allotment and you will provide a way of determining their successful completion.

4.5 – Brand Positioning Strategy

Brand positioning strategy refers to how you will achieve, demonstrate or present your method of branding to the customer and how you intend to achieve the results you desire.

The following are the methods to be considered to effectively allow you to reach these goals.

1. **Defensive Strategy** - This occurs if you are a leader and wish to maintain your position.

2. **Offensive Strategy** - This occurs if you are not the leader and wish to move up or be the leader.

3. **Flanking Strategy** - This employs focusing on an unchallenged area, using the element of surprise and carrying out a relentless pursuit.

4. **Guerrilla Strategy** - This is where you serve a niche, remain focused and flexible and use hit and run tactics to take over the competitor's position.

4.6 – Brand Slogans and Jingles

Branding slogans and jingle have achieved many successes over the years. Implementation of a successful slogan or jingle can create a household name or industry standard for an offering.

Many marketers have achieved greatness with a single slogan or jingle. Finding one to suit your personality or business could create additional attention to your products or services.

Building a service brand by successful results and happy customers is the best start but adding a slogan or a jingle can put the icing on the cake for you.

Make sure a slogan or jingle it is one that is liked and not offensive or libelous. Test market it with a select few trusted friends or customers first before you release it. You just need to think of some products or services to see how slogans or Jingles have been successful. We often take that association for granted.

Who do you think of for the following?

- **For Products** – Headache tablets, Camping equipment

- **For Services** – Car rental, Cash loans

- **For Corporate** – Shoes for the sports industry, Computers or mobile phones

- **For Personal** – King of Rock, King of Pop

For every one of these topics someone has made an impact on our conscious and sub-conscious thought process through Branding.

4.7 – Brand Changing

Rule of Branding - Most important is to make sure you can deliver what you promise.

In the process of Branding many companies have made promises before they are sure they can deliver. There can be nothing more devastating to branding than one's inability to deliver its promise.

Do not create a brand identity, vision or mission and then forget about them never to revisit again. Always make sure that all areas in your company continue to reflect what you are trying to accomplish in your brand marketing process.

If your branding is not doing the proper job, then consider what you are doing to achieve it or as a last resort consider revising it.

Re-creation can be very dangerous as it can either add new life or it can greatly harm your business image.

4.8 – Branding Recommendations Summary

Branding recommendations are the steps that you will take to achieve your branding goals.

You will list and discuss these recommendations in Part 5.0 Final. - Review and Selection of Objectives.

5.0 – Final Review and Selection of Objectives

In this section, you will review all the recommendations from the previous component sections and make a final list of Objectives for your marketing plan.

Review Areas

1. Business Summary
2. Situation Analysis
3. Marketing Strategy
4. Branding

6.0 –Integrated Marketing Communications Plan (IMCP)

The Integrated Marketing Communications plan (IMCP) will bring together all your advertising ideas to work together in harmony.

IMC is the short form for **Integrated Marketing Communications** which is the advertising process whereby all aspects of advertising are designed to work together as opposed to working independently.

The P part of IMCP is Your Plan to achieve this.

Your Plan

This will bring together everything that you have researched, and thought about, and written about.

It will be a plan to blend all advertising and promotions and allow you to achieve all your visions and goals.

You will know your target markets and the advertising vehicles that will be used for each one. Keep a good cross section and balance of free and cost incurred vehicles.

Note: It is important to create this as a separate file as well as being part of your budget and Implementation Schedule.

When viewed as a separate document it will provide easier reference and allow you to stay focused in your advertising agenda.

IMC Strategy refers to how the marketer will implement his plans to achieve this teamwork effect in their advertising process. It will outline the objectives and how they will achieve each of these objectives.

7.0 – Marketing Budget

The Marketing Plan Budget (MPB) will allocate the funds that you will set aside to accomplish your marketing plans. This will be done as part of your financial plan for your business.

In this budget, you should include all the areas that will allow you to implement your marketing plan and build on it and providing your basis for future growth.

Budget Item Examples

1. **Objectives and Tactics** – any tactical undertakings such as adding your web site URL to all your business forms.

2. **IMCP – Integrated Marketing Communications Plan** – List all the advertising vehicles you intend to use. Provide an annual budget allowance for each vehicle or activity. Show the free ones also.

    o   **Trade Shows** – Show trade shows you will participate in or attend as a visitor - date and duration.

    o   **Further Research and Education** – This will apply to further education for yourself, your employees, your suppliers and customers.

    o   **Office equipment and supplies** – Show any new equipment you will need to add to implement your plan.

    o   **Brand development** – an amount to achieve your brand goals

    o   **Client maintenance** – add an amount to maintain your existing clientele such as entertainment, golf tournament.

8.0 – Implementation Schedule for Marketing Plan

This part will be done last after your budget and integrated marketing plan. It will list all your final undertakings resulting from discussions from every part of your marketing plan outline. It will be lengthy perhaps 12 or more pages.

It is best to design this to be dealt with or executed in stages (quarterly) so that you are not overwhelmed with too many different undertakings at once. Arrange your implementation plan so that as many of the most important things can be done first.

S3 – MARKETING PLAN CREATION

In the previous chapter, we provided an explanation for each component in your marketing plan, so that you understand what each part is and does.

In this chapter, we will provide you with the questions and means to create your Marketing Plan. Once this part is completed you will be ready to begin the Implementation of the marketing plan that you have created.

1.0 – Business Summary

To create your Business Summary, answer the following questions in parts 1.1 to 1.3.

1.1 - Starting Day Summary

1. When was, the business started and who started it?
2. List your companies starting financial business partners.
3. Outline your starting Target Markets.
4. Customer base - who, where and why you started with them?
5. List your starting products and/or services from best to least.
6. The perceived benefits of your offerings (yours and clients)
7. Initial suppliers and how they assisted the starting efforts
8. What were your advertising methods - from best to least?
9. Did you have any thoughts for Branding? List them.
10. What was your starting sales force?
11. What were your projected sales for year one?

1.2 - The Journey Summary

1. List any management changes that occurred and why?
2. Did your financial partners change - when and why?
3. If any changes occurred to the original target markets – when and why did, they change?
4. Were these changes good or bad for the company? Explain.
5. Did your customer demographics (profile) change and why?
6. List additions of any products or services and why?
7. List deletions of any products or services and why?
8. List changes to your suppliers, when and why they occurred?
9. What changes occurred in your advertising - why or why not?
10. What changes occurred to your sales force and why/why not?

11. Did you meet your projected sales targets? If yes or no say why?

12. Many good ideas are often forgotten and left behind.

    a. Often this review can rekindle them

1.3 - Present Day Summary

1. Is there any ownership or a management change being considered?

2. Are there changes in financial partners being considered? Why?

3. Are you considering any new target markets? If so where & why?

4. Are any changes being considered for your customer base?

5. Are your present-day products and/or services, and their perceived benefits working for you? How well?

6. Are any new products or services being considered?

7. Who manages the sales department and why?

8. What prospecting methods and promotions are you using?

9. Are existing Advertising Methods and promotions working?

10. Is there and existing Budget for advertising and promotion?

11. Are you considering any changes to your present Sales force?

12. Are you satisfied with present Sales figures?

13. Is there a sales plan or Marketing Strategy of any kind in place?

14. Do you have a Branding Strategy?

1.4 – Recommendations for Improvement

You have now completed a review of your company's history from starting point to present day. In this reflection, you may see changes that might or should take place because of this review.

Make a list of ideas for improvement from this exercise for review in section 5.0 of **S3 Marketing Plan Creation,** where you will turn these ideas into Objectives for implementation in your Marketing Plan.

2.0 – Situation Analysis

2.1.0 – Your Company 2.1.1to 2.1.7

Your situation analysis will examine your company based on established marketing plan concepts. Each part will have its own unique benefit for your plan.

2.1.1 - S.W.O.T. Analysis - Use the following ideas as a start and add your own.

List your Company "Strengths"

- Do you have a strong sales department, service department, or delivery service, etc.? Explain what they are and why you feel they are strengths and are important for your success?

- List the strengths of your offerings (products and your services). List all their features and benefits to the customer and why you feel they are important for your success?

- Do you have a strategically located business that will attract new customers easily?

- Do you have an excellent cash position that allows you to choose competitive purchasing or get payment discounts?

List your company "Weaknesses"

- Employee weaknesses - Explain what they are and why you feel their weaknesses are interfering with your potential success?

- Do you have a lower quality in your product or service offerings than your competitors?

- Are you considered overpriced? Why?

- Is your location a weakness in attracting new customers?

- Do you have a poor cash position that prevents you from choosing good sourcing or taking payment discounts?

List the "Opportunities" that you see for your company

Look at existing and future potential as far as opportunities and list them. Give this much thought and do research on the possibilities. This is a start and other sections will expand these ideas.

1. What new target markets can you look at or add?

2. What new products/services can you develop or add?

3. Are there new uses for existing products and services?

4. Are there any new government regulations creating more needs for your offerings?

    Example: Increased environmental control.

5. Should you consider any relocation or expansion opportunities?

6. Are there any areas available for cost reduction?

7. Are there any government incentives in making improvements in your own business or in the selling of your products or services such as: *"Energy Incentives for gas or electrical savings?"*

8. Are there any government assisted hiring programs you can use to cut overheads and bring in extra help or higher caliber people?

9. Can you share advertising costs with suppliers?

List the "Threats" that you see for your company.

1. Is your present marketplace for products or services shrinking? If so, why is this happening?

2. Are there new competitors that are taking away business due to price or other reasons? Explain?

3. Do you have the possible loss of any key employees that you can still prevent?

4. Are there threats of increased costs from suppliers? Where and why? Can they be prevented? How?

5. Are advertising sources talking about increasing their costs? Do you have any alternative back-up sources?

6. Do you have a fleet of service trucks that need maintenance or replacing?

2.1.2 – Your Company's Macro Environment

Your Macro Environment refers to the internal and external forces that you cannot change but must adapt to; whereas, the results of the SWOT analysis show changes that are within your ability to control.

Outline all the areas you see in your Macro Environment.

Examples

1. New government regulations that negatively affect your services or products such as - very restrictive environmental issues or new licensing controls for your services

2. An influx of goods from offshore that offer much lower prices.

3. Increasing prices for natural gas and electricity and the increase of transportation fuels for sales people, and service trucks.

4. Elimination of government incentive programs for your products, services such as energy incentives for your customers.

5. Loss of business due to customer closures or moving

6. Retirement of buyers who favor your products and services

7. New customer policies that increase your costs of product handling, delivery or packaging

8. A Key employee has left and formed their own company and has taken some important clients with them

You may have no control in preventing their occurrences or implementation; but, you can reduce the negative impact on your business by facing them and finding solutions to handle them.

Make an open-ended list of changes and ways to adapt to them.

They will be continuously reviewed and made into Objectives in 5.0

2.1.3- Your Products and Services Offerings

a) List all your products and services that represent everything you offer your customers and potential clients outlining their:

- Benefits

- Features

- Weaknesses

b) Make a list of your suppliers and sub-contracted services listing all the people and departments that you work with while servicing your customers such as:

1. Owner/General Manager

2. Sales Manager

3. Sales or Service representatives

4. Project Managers

5. Installation crews

6. Purchasing, Order Desk

7. Expediting, Shipping

8. Service department and Customer relations

How are these people affecting your ability to provide optimum service and quality to your customers?

Examples

- Is reaction time to your requests excellent, just OK or slow?

- Are they efficient or are there a lot of mistakes?

- Is the quality of their offerings excellent, just OK or poor?

- How is their pricing and does it affect getting orders?

- Do they correct their mistakes willingly without extra costs?

Make a list of ways to improve your products, service and your supplier relations and show how you feel these recommendations will help.

They will be reviewed and made into Objectives in 5.0

2.1.4 - Customer Base

1. Make a complete list of your existing customers

2. Rate and group each of them for the following

  - **Sales volume** – show actual annual

  - **Profitability** – high, average, low

  - **Relationship** – easy, average or hard to please

  - **Loyalty is based on** – service, quality, price, not known

  - **Referrals** – do they provide them? How many? Why or why not?

  - **Growth potential** – provide percentage

3. Answer these questions

  - How did they become your customer?

  - What are their demographic characteristics?

  - Income bracket, Company size or type

  - Age bracket of clients, individuals or companies

  - Client type: Household, Commercial, Industrial, Automotive

  - Needs that are unique

From this exercise, you should see how you obtained these people as customers, why they are remaining customers and why they may or may not be the type of prospect you wish to pursue.

List all the characteristics that are common to your preferred customer base, because these are the traits that you need to look for in new prospects or even possibly avoid.

Your List Details

  1. List the non-preferred traits as well so you can set some boundaries or standards of service.

  2. List what other types of businesses or consumers could also fall under the same or even similar list of traits.

     They will be reviewed and made into Objectives in 5.0

2.1.5 - Geographical Boundaries

Answer the following

1. Does your market have a certain reach?

2. Is there a restriction or are there boundary limitation (border, river, mountain, railway tracks)?

Consumers will usually have a radius that they will travel within, to obtain certain products or services. For businesses that have their products delivered, the geographical limits will usually be extended.

Time not distance is your enemy. Look at how you can reduce delivery times. Examine how you can overcome boundaries with good delivery and can brag about it. Make it a feature.

Some questions about your Geographical Boundaries

a. Are you overextending these boundaries, creating extra costs?

b. Are you restricting your focus because of geographical limits?

c. Does your advertising ignore boundaries that increases costs?

d. Is your advertising creating artificial boundaries and decreasing your potential target market?

e. What are you doing that is limiting your ability to reach your full market potential in your area?

f. Could you be doing something to adjust your boundaries to achieve their best potential?

g. It could be getting your own smaller delivery truck for small rush shipments. Your express service

   - It might mean looking at different shipping providers
   - It might mean hiring more service or sales people
   - It could be changing your boundaries

Make a list of all the areas that could improve problems in your present approach to Geographical Boundaries.

They will be reviewed and made into Objectives in 5.0

2.1.6 - Present Market Position

What position do you think you hold in the marketplace as far as sales volume or image when compared to your competition?

- List all competition and compare

- What position do you feel your customers see you in?

- How does this affect your sales efforts?

    List recommendations for improvement for review in 5.0

2.1.7 – Analysis of Sales and Service

If you have a separate service department, sales department or have managers looking after your service or sales representatives, it is a good idea to get input from all of them.

The sales and service representatives are on the front lines and get the reactions of customers and potential customers first hand. Their input will often reveal how well any marketing, advertising or branding is being accepted in the marketplace.

If you have purchasing, accounting, estimating or advertising people that also play a role in obtaining sales and achieving profitability they also should be involved.

Some initial ideas to consider for review

1. Are the estimating methods accurate or up to date?

2. Are estimates provided on a timely basis to keep the sales momentum, or do clients cool off while waiting for them?

3. Is the sales internal infrastructure friendly, efficient and enthusiastic when dealing with customers?

4. Is your order desk, expediting and shipping accurate, responsive and service oriented?

5. How quickly and efficiently does your company respond to mistakes?

    a. Is there a follow up after corrections are made?

    b. Who does it?

    c. Is this information given to management?

6. Are your suppliers and sub-trades providing competitive rates and the kind of service you are happy with?

7. Are your offerings sold and viewed based on quality, or are sales mostly because of lower prices?

8. Are your advertising vehicles achieving the results you want?

9. Are your promotional materials attractive, attention-getting, informative, focused and effective?

10. Do your terms and conditions create problems in obtaining orders? If so – where and what can be done to resolve this?

11. Do customers view delivery as excellent, OK or too Slow

12. How are your procedures for pricing issues resolved?

    a. Do you have an efficient and effective way to react quickly to pricing when an order is in the balance?

    b. Who has the authority to lower prices?

13. How are Sales targets established and how are they received by your sales reps?

14. Are there any ideas for Branding?

15. Is there sufficient support from the company regarding Marketing and advertising and what recommendations can be made for improvement?

16. Are the sales and service people quick to respond to inquiries or requests from your office or clients?

17. Do you have an effective process for sales or service to keep everyone informed with new ideas or tips in improving things?

Make a list of recommendations

They will be reviewed and made into Objectives in 5.0

2.2.0 – Your Competition 2.2.1 to 2.2.7

For your competition situation analysis, you will examine your competition in a similar way as you did for your own company analysis.

List all your competitors by name.

Examples

- Seeking customers with the same demographics

- Offering the same or similar products and services

- Meeting the same or similar needs as you say you do

Include

1. The company name, Address, Telephone number fax or email addresses that are available for head office and any branches they have that could affect your marketing efforts.

2. Web site(s) and Social media connections

3. Show the key personnel including

    a. Owner

    b. CEO

    c. General Manager

(List Continued)

    d. Sales manager, Service Manager

    e. Sales and service representative and their territories

    f. Order desk personnel

2.2.1 - SWOT Analysis of each Competitor

Provide a detailed list of the Strengths and Weaknesses, the Opportunities and Threats for each of your competitors from an overall company image, reputation, products, services and Suppliers.

Outline Opportunities showing how you can overcome their strong points and capitalize on their weak points **for 5.0 objectives**

2.2.2 - Macro Environment of each competitor

What Macro Environmental factors face your competitors that you could capitalize on and outline how you can use these factors to your advantage? **Review and establish objectives in 5.0**

2.2.3 - Products and Services of each

- Show everything, they offer – not just products and services like your own – but what they have that you do not have.

- List any potential additions to your offerings needed to match or to do more for your existing and potential customers that your competitor's existing offerings are presently doing.

- Provide a detailed explanation or description for each outlining their Brand names and who their suppliers are.

Your answers will be reviewed and made into Objectives in 5.0

2.2.4 - Customer base of each

- Is it the same customer base or is it smaller or larger than yours?
- Are there any examples here that you could benefit from?
- Do your share part of the business with any customers?

Your answers will be reviewed and made into Objectives in 5.0

2.2.5 - Geographical Boundaries of each

- Are they the same boundaries as your company?
- Are they better located than you?
- How can you better handle your area to compete?

Your answers will be reviewed and made into Objectives in 5.0

2.2.6 - Present Market position of each

Describe where you see each of your competitor's position regarding overall market share and customer perception.

- How do you feel your customers see them?

- What you think their percentage share of the market is.

- Look at ways to improve your position - increase your share.

Make a list of recommendations for 5.0 Objectives

2.2.7 – Analysis of their sales/service department

Outline how effective you feel each of your competitor's sales and service departments are

- Are they represented by people with better sales or service skills?

- Is their infrastructure better or worse than yours for client support?

- Do they have better sales or order desk personnel?

- Are they better equipped with service trucks or personnel?

- What improvements are required by your company?

- Where you can outperform them?
  Make a list of recommendations for 5.0 Objectives

3.0 – Marketing Strategy

Everything you have done to this point is essential for planning your Marketing Strategy. The knowledge you will now have about yourself and your competition will allow you to now make informed decisions about what you can do in this section.

3.1 - Marketing Vision

This is what you want and expect your market position to be by a certain time and what you want and expect your efforts to achieve?

Some Ideas

- What do you expect your products and services will be?

- Who do you see as your potential customers?

- What do you see as your geographical boundaries?

- What will your market position be?

- What will be your target markets?

- What other visions or desires do you have?

Summarize and make a list of recommendations

For your 5.0 Objectives

3.2 - Marketing Mission

Your marketing mission is the journey you will take to achieve your vision.

- Make a list of what your mission objectives could be.

- What will your company do to achieve your vision?

- Suggest deadlines and who might become responsible for its implementation and achievement.

Make a list of mission recommendations for 5.0 objectives

3.3 – Marketing Goals

Your goals will be the tangible targets that you have set for your products and services in your marketing efforts. Your vision will be achieved by your mission.

They will include the methods you will use to get there and the date by which you will accomplish your goals.

- List all your ideas for establishing goals for marketing strategy that you are now using.

- List what you see as your new marketing goals for discussion.

- List what you see as your future marketing goals for discussion.

- What areas need immediate attention to improve your ability to reach your goals?

Some examples of Immediate goals

- Increase outside sales representation by 2 people.

- Add one inside order desk sales person.

- Add one service truck to your service department.

- Add a delivery van this year for small rush orders to lower your shipping costs of large trucks and shorten delivery times.

Some examples of Future Goals

- Double your geographical area within two years - Give details.

- Add three sales representatives in two years.

- Add a total of three more service trucks in three years.

Make a list of recommendations for 5.0 Objectives

3.4 - Target Markets - Clearly outline what your target markets are and could be as shown in 3.4.1 to 3.4.3

3.4.1 - Growth Markets - List the types of customers and offerings that are providing you with MOST of your existing business.

- Who are they and why are they your customers?

- What percentage of their business do you have presently?

- With a determined effort, how much could you increase your existing sales percentage/dollars with any of these customers?

- Is there an increased demand for any products or services in your area?   If so, where and why is that happening?

- Are there any new uses for any product lines or services that could increase sales for you?

- Have you approached any of these growth markets yet?

- How many similar potential prospects have not yet been approached?

- How much (percentage) could these growth markets add to your existing sales?

Make a list of recommendations for 5.0 Objectives.

3.4.2 - New Markets: - List where your existing offerings could help clients in new ways:

Examples

- Save office operating costs of lighting, heating, air conditioning

- Save shipping costs – different packaging, higher volumes

- Save process costs – reduction of time, materials, energy

- Reduce space – more efficient equipment

- Replace old technology – reduce manpower or energy

- Provide environmentally friendly features – bio chemicals

- Replace existing methods that are dangerous, harmful to work with and are creating safety issues. - Non-flammable cleaning

Other Ideas

- Look for other needs that you can solve and add to this list

- List new companies or markets where these same products or services could apply.

- List where you feel your experience in your industry could make it possible for you to offer training or consulting in certain tasks of your target markets.

- Show where and how you can add any of these processes or products to your customer base.

  Make a list of recommendations for 5.0 Objectives

3.4.3 - New Product development - Make a list of any products or services that you are developing or have developed and are available for distribution.

Some examples

- Your Company has just developed a new chemistry to handle a process that will reduce health risks.

- Your company has a new type of product to cut operating costs for a process.

- You may own intellectual property and can now introduce the chemistry or product to your existing customer base and beyond by offering distribution rights to others outside your area.

- Could you become the exclusive distributor for a company that has just done the above?

- Are there new products or services that are available to add to your existing offerings to create a more complete package?

- Are there any exclusive distribution rights that no one else has in your area that will compliment your existing lineup?

  Make a list of recommendations for 5.0 Objectives

3.5 – Marketing Positioning Strategy

Based on what you see and what you feel your customers and prospects see as your present market position including any goals you have set; what positioning strategy best suits your recommendations?

Outline and clearly identify where you want to be. Decide what you need to do to reach your desired position and how you will know when you have reached it.

Strategy Options

1. **Defensive** – If you are # 1 and want to remain there
2. **Offensive** – If you are not # 1 and want to move up
3. **Flanking** – If you want to go after an unchallenged area
4. **Guerilla** – If you want to take over a competitor's niche

Make a list of recommendations for 5.0 Objectives

3.6 – Advertising Vehicles

We have listed many examples of advertising in Part 1. Researching these different types of advertising will provide the basis for discussion.

If you can, assign this research to individuals who will have a vested interest in the outcome such as accounting, sales or service.

As an owner or manager, you should also be "hands on" in this research even if it involves others.

Set a time frame to do a preliminary research of all or as many types as you possibly can. Once the time has elapsed hold additional meetings to discuss and decide which forms of advertising might be considered.

Repeat this until you have a full list of advertising methods that you can use. Establish as many free sources as possible.

Make a list of recommendations for 5.0 Objectives

3.7 – Marketing Mix

The marketing mix can be covered with the 7 P's Products, Price, Place, Promotion, People, Process, and Physical evidence. If you make certain claims in your advertising, your offerings must clearly demonstrate that your claims are true in each of the 7 P components.

It will be up to you to determine your approach to promoting each area. Select the positive attributes that show why each P will benefit the customer and outline how you will do this.

Marketing mix survey (7 P's)– How best can you present each?

1. Products (and Services) – Outline what your main products/services will be and the main features and/or benefits that you will use when you are advertising your offerings. Outline how you will demonstrate the reality of your claim.

2. Price – Review your quality, estimating methods and your market position to enforce how you will approach this topic. Establish what you will say about your prices.

If you say your price is affordable – it must be affordable to your target market.

If your offerings are higher priced than much of your competition, can you show that your prices reflect higher quality or performance? – Do so in your promotions.

This will also be achieved in the Branding Process.

3. Place (Geographical location) – Decide what your statement will be about your location. If you say you are conveniently located – it must be convenient to your target market.

If you are not conveniently located, then stress how you have overcome this with your superior delivery service. Show how your location has created a positive benefit for your customers.

4. Promotion (Advertising Vehicles) – make sure your advertising methods will allow you to demonstrate all your claims clearly. Use the right advertising to make your point.

Do not make false or misleading claims to attract clients, because they will soon be discovered and do more harm than any promotion can achieve.

5. People – Decide what you will say about your people that will enhance your marketing strategy.

If you say your people are friendly - they must be friendly. If you say they are knowledgeable– they must be.

Set in motion a training program to instill these traits in any of your employees who have any dealings with your customers.

6. Process – If you have a process that can be promoted in your marketing make sure it is consistent with your claim. It could be quality control, expediting, or shipping etc.

7. Physical Evidence – Be prepared to provide solid physical evidence for all your claims.

Example: If you say that your gym is well equipped – take pictures, make a video or provide a list the equipment c/w all their features.

The proof of all your claims should be readily seen in your advertising and branding and can be immediately experienced by your customers.

Make a list for discussion in 5.0. Describe what you are doing or will do to achieve all your claims that you made for the Seven P's.

3.8 – Sales/Service Strategies

In what ways, can the sales/service representatives be assisted by the company/marketing to make their job more effective and increase efficiency, improve closing ratios and increase profits?

Some Example areas to consider – add your own

Traits or key elements that will help you achieve better results in the selling process?

- Respect, Enthusiasm, Product knowledge

- What prospecting methods are working the best and why?

- What prospecting methods are ineffective and why?

- Are there methods where the company could provide more assistance to sales and improve leads or closing ratios?

- Advertising, Supplier input, Training Seminars

- How can the company help create better sales presentations?

  o More involvement, better facilities

  o Breakfast or lunch seminars

  o Sales aids better brochures

  o Equipment that could make a difference

    ▪ Audio or video equipment

  o Web site make-over, or creation of one

- What Closing methods seem to work better than others?

- What are the most common objections that prevent getting the order? Why are they happening?

- Outline the ways in which these objections are being overcome.

- What advertising methods are getting the most leads?

Make a list of all recommendations from 3.1 to 3.8 for 5.0 objectives

4.0- Branding

This part could be broken into longer time allowances as branding can often take more time to prepare and implement than the initial components of a marketing plan.

Keep the goals and timelines of each step of your branding plan short enough to see and control your progress.

Branding will provide an identity and perceived added value for your company, your products and services.

Branding will reflect how well you know your company and its offerings and can deliver that identity to the conscious level of the customer.

The knowledge is usually there

But sometimes it takes a while

To express it the way you see it and feel it

Some Benefits

Branding will provide a focal point and a base from which you can work to create greater loyalty with your existing customers and build confidence in your prospects mind.

Branding will help you attain the market position and recognition that you desire as seen in your vision and goals.

Branding is perhaps the most important thing that you can do to "allow" the resulting success of your efforts.

Because branding can become so important to your success; do not rush through it or leave it behind because it presents a challenge.

If you have difficulty making these decisions

1. You should establish any unfinished part of this section as an undertaking in your marketing plan to complete in the best time frame possible.

2. Do not become indifferent by allowing too much time.

3. A little pressure to produce your Branding - is good.

4. Break the process into sections with certain parts to be completed each week or by the end of the month.

5. Do not put your marketing plan on hold while you tackle Branding

Keep your branding consistent!

Whether it is your business cards, your logo, your letterhead, your product labeling, your web site, the sign in front of your office, your service trucks; keep it consistent.

Just as in your Advertising, there is nothing worse for your Branding Identity than to have multiple signals going out to your customers or prospects. It will confuse them and your messages to them.

Although it may not appear to be significant on the surface, people do not like mixed signals even if it is in their sub-consciousness (which is the normal place for these thoughts).

In confusing them you will create doubt in your ability to provide continuous quality in your services and products.

It is usually when a critical situation occurs that these mixed feeling will surface and do you the most harm.

The confusion and doubt will lead to lack of trust and some existing clients will jump ship as soon as the first problem arises, and new prospects will be reluctant to give you their business.

Brand Perception

A brand perception creates reality and exemplifies a feeling of trust, security and confidence and resides mostly in one's subconscious. This added value fulfills both functional and emotional needs that will demonstrate superior qualities over your competition.

You must do the research that will determine who your target audience will be. You must know how you want them to perceive your brand and what position you occupy in the marketplace.

The trust created by a brand; builds loyal customers, and a base for your sales and service people to depend on for reference.

4.1– Brand Identity

Branding gives your company, product or services its own attributes, a personality and enforces expected results. A brand identity becomes reality and exemplifies a feeling of trust, security and confidence.

Most of all, it will provide

An identity separate from that of your competition

Steps for your Brand Identity

The most important factor is to maintain the quality of the brand name with each new product introduced.

All existing products must remain consistent or they all may be affected; especially as seen by those new consumers or companies that are just emerging into the marketplace.

What to do

- Provide a description of how you see your type of branding as it applies to your company. Choose from the list of types below

- Provide a description of your concepts to recommend their incorporation into your marketing plan.

- List unanswered items so that they will become undertakings.

- You will show them as an undertaking in your branding objectives until you can find the right answer.

Type 1 - Product Branding

- Start a list of possible trade names for your products.

- If you feel you are NOT ready to establish a trade name for your offerings, make it an undertaking to finish within one to three months or sooner.

- Place this undertaking into your objectives for Branding.

Answer these questions.

1. What do we offer that is different/better than our competitors?

2. How will our customers benefit? What's in it for them?

3. Why should our customers trust us?

4. How will our products track record exemplify the brand?

5. What will they see because of accepting our brand promise?

Type 2 - Service Branding

- Start a list of possible trade names for your Services.

- Services can be a more difficult area to control simply because they may depend on the efforts of many different individuals or outlets.

Answer these questions

1. What do we offer that is different, better than our competition?

2. How will our customers benefit? What's in it for them?

3. Why should our customers trust us?

4. How will our service track record exemplify the brand?

5. What will they see because of accepting our brand promise?

Type 3 - Corporate or Business Branding

Start a list of ways you would like your business or corporate identity to be seen.

Answer these Questions

1. Who are we?

2. What do we represent to ourselves?

3. What do we represent to our customers?

4. Why should our customers believe in us?

5. What makes us different from our competition?

6. What makes us better and how?

7. Look at your marketing strategy for more ideas

8. Keep asking until your Identity is clear

Type 4 - Personal Branding or Identity

Answer these questions

1. Who am I?

2. What do I represent in my offerings?

3. What do I represent to my customers?

4. Why should customers believe in my name?

5. What makes me different from the competition?

6. What makes my offerings better?

7. Look at your marketing strategy for more ideas.

8. Keep asking until your Identity is clear

Make a list of Brand Identity recommendations for 5.0 Objectives

4.2 – Brand Vision

Once stated publicly your brand vision becomes a commitment to yourself, your customers, potential customers, to your employees and suppliers.

Describe what you see your branding process will achieve for:

- Yourself

- Your company and employees

- Your offerings (products/services)

- Your suppliers

- Your customers

- Your competition

Make a list of recommendations for 5.0 Brand Vision Objectives

4.3 – Brand Mission

What is the process, objectives or steps that you will take to achieve your brand vision?

- Outline how the vision will be achieved.

- State in detail the person(s) or group(s) who could be responsible for carrying out this mission or various parts of it.

- What is the time frame to complete the mission?

- How will you know when it is achieved?

Make a list of recommendations for 5.0 Brand Mission Objectives

4.4 – Branding Goals

Your branding goals are your destination points that you are looking to achieve.

- Make a list of your possible goals.
    - Put in order of importance to be completed
- List the ways of how you could achieve them.
- List what your target dates are for each goal.
- How will you know when you have achieved them?

Make a list of recommendations for 5.0 Branding goals Objectives

4.5 – Brand Positioning Strategy

Brand positioning strategy refers to how you will achieve, demonstrate or present your method of branding to the customer and how you intend to obtain the results you desire.

To Achieve this, you will

- Evaluate your present market position.

- Your Goal will comprise of where you want to see yourself within a certain time element such as 1 to 3 years or in 5 years, why you want to be there and how you will get there.

- Be specific about what the Goal or goals are.

Which of the following positioning strategies will you use and explain how and why?

> **Defensive Strategy** - This occurs if you are a leader and wish to maintain your position.
>
> **Offensive Strategy** - This occurs if you are not the leader and wish to move up or be the leader.
>
> **Flanking Strategy** - These employs focusing on an unchallenged area, using the element of surprise and carrying out relentless pursuit.
>
> **Guerrilla Strategy** - This is where you serve a niche, remain focused and flexible and use hit and run tactics to take over the competitor's position.
>
> **Product Position** - This is how a product is perceived when compared to a competitor's product.

Outline your ideas for your strategy showing different ways that you can achieve your goals for your 5.0 Objectives

4.6 – Branding Slogans and Jingles

One way to get employees involved is to hold a contest with a reward for those slogans or jingles chosen for consideration and testing and then a grand prize for the final one(s) selected.

If you wish to widen the scope you can include customers or even involve social media to make people more aware of your company.

People like contests and it could even increase sales and obtain new customers with people testing your products or services to be able to enter their ideas in the contest - but the actual purchasing of your offerings should not be a condition to take part.

- Have someone outline your contest rules and regulations.
- Set a deadline for your first ideas and test market them.
- Choose the most successful.
- Make the prize-winning presentation an event to remember.

By expanding it to the outside world, you will probably need to make the prize much bigger than if it is only an internal contest.

Do not try something that will have an adverse effect on your image or reputation.

If you cannot do it right – keep it just within your company

Make a list of recommendations for 5.0 Slogans/Jingles Objectives

4.7 – Brand Changing

Steps to consider if a change is made in branding

1. Make it a smooth transition because people hate change.
2. Characterize your re-branding process and give it a human element of a reason for change such as maturing or growing.
3. Make it appear to be a progressive change for the better – a positive move.

List of recommendations for discussion in 5.0 Objectives

5.0 – Final Review and Selection of Objectives

You will now be ready to create your marketing plan based on all your answers from 1.0 Business Summary to 4.7 Brand Changing.

What you create here will form the list of Objectives for the final drafting of your Marketing Plan.

It is important to have everyone with a vested interest involved in these final discussions as valuable input can come from many directions.

It also creates a team spirit and helps enforce the Company Vision, Mission and Goals.

Note: Some parts of the Business summary may be proprietary and not suitable for some for your employees to see. Make a list of non-proprietary items for discussion.

From this list of Objectives, you will create the last three parts of your Marketing Plan which are

1. - IMCP Integrated Marketing Communications Plan

2. - Marketing Plan Budget

3. - Implementation Schedule

Items for Establishment of Objectives

- **Business Summary** – From your recommendations, select your final objectives for this section and list them in order of importance.

- **Situation Analysis** – From your recommendations, select your final objectives for this section and list them in order of importance.

- **Marketing Strategy** – From your recommendations, select your final objectives for this section and list them in order of importance.

- **Branding** – From your recommendations, select your final objectives for this section and list them in order of importance.

Final Drafting of your Plan

6.0 – Integrated Marketing Communications Plan

Preparation

In the earlier part of your undertakings, you have completed your market summary and studied your competition; you have also listed your present offerings and the future offerings that you will introduce to your existing target markets.

You have also identified your growth markets and the new markets you wish to pursue. You have decided on your Marketing strategy and completed your review of branding and outlined these areas for your marketing plan.

You have researched the different vehicles available for your advertising and promotion of your products and services. You have outlined them for your Marketing and Branding Strategies and have established what advertising you will use.

You have established a Sales Plan with a list of undertakings

Time for Action

It is now time to put together your IMC Plan. This will bring together everything that you have researched, and thought about, and written about.

It will be a plan to blend all advertising and promotions that will allow you to achieve all your visions and goals effectively and efficiently.

Do a separate plan just for the IMCP as well as including the undertakings in your Implementation Plan.

Describe your IMC strategy

- Make a list of all the advertising vehicles you intend to use.
- Indicate which target market each vehicle will be used for.
- Include both free methods and ones that will have a cost.
- Provide a full description of each method and why chosen.
    - Provide an item cost for each method.

- o State when and where you intend to use each.
  - o If they are time sensitive such as trade shows indicate when they are scheduled and for how long.
- When you are done, you will have a full list for your Budget.

This is the final discussion area for what will be included in your Budget and Implementation Schedule

7.0 – Marketing Plan Budget

Your existing cash position, Projected Sales, Pricing and Profitability will usually set the scope of your marketing plan budget. Use as many free promotional items as you can.

Prepare a full list of items you will use to achieve your marketing plan goals. This can be broken down into components to fit the timeline of your Implementation schedule.

We have created a sample Budget on the next page to give you an idea of what it should look like.

You will; of course, have different components in your own budget that are relevant to your own business.

Sample Annual Marketing Budget

Description	Budget Amount
Web site	
Design	$ 1,600
Support software	$ 800
Webinars	$ 1,200
Social Media	
Design	$ 2,450
Advertising	$ 4,800
Paid Traditional Advertising	
Trade shows	$ 3,500
Trade Publications	$ 3,000
Newspaper (help wanted)	$ 1,000
Other	$ 2,000
Internally generated	
Direct mail	$ 1,500
Office equipment and supplies	
Equipment, furniture	$ 3,500
Office supplies, brochures	$ 3,200
Client Maintenance	
Socializing, expenses	$ 6,200
Brand development	
Merchandising, promotions	$ 3,000
Educational Programs	
Morning meetings	$ 2,500
TOTAL	$40,250

S4 – PLAN IMPLEMENTATION

8.0 – Implementation Schedule

List all the undertakings or Objectives that you have elected to do in 5.0 - Objectives, 6.0 your IMCP and 7.0 Marketing Plan Budget.

Arrange these undertakings into their order of implementation based on importance and budgeting. Group them quarterly for execution.

Try to start with as many free and low-cost items while balancing importance with cost to avoid budget overtaxing at the front end. This allows you to build on your successes.

We have suggested who might look after implementation of these undertakings only to provide this sample implementation schedule.

Based on qualifications of your own employees you will; of course, designate the people you feel best suited for each of the tasks.

The components and undertaking will also be different as they will reflect your own company's offerings and business model.

Sample partial plan - First Quarter

Undertakings

Item 1 – Begin weekly office meetings

1. Establish agenda and implement weekly meetings starting week 2

Item 2 – Website

1. Establish a project leader and group to include Sales/Marketing/Office Manager
2. Review existing website and compare to competitor's sites
3. Prepare an initial list of recommendations to discuss
4. Provide list of undertakings by end of week 2
5. Have site manager begin implementation by end of week 3
6. Complete by end of week 4

Item 3 – Newsletter

1. Start week 2
2. Appoint someone to do rough design and the page layout.
3. Have the sales manager make a list of topics for presentation and do a short write up for each.
4. Have Marketing and Sales departments make a list of features and benefits of the company and our products.
5. Have the office manager provide a draft for approval by me.
6. Decide how this will be sent. Will it be email, regular mail or both.
7. Introduce the newsletter to our existing customers by the end of the fourth week

Item 4 – Join Social sites

1. Assign a project leader (sales or marketing department) to start research immediately.
2. Project manager and I will decide the parameters of the social sites
3. Start research beginning of week two

4. Complete research by end of week 3 and hold a meeting at that time to discuss findings.

5. Select the initial sites to join and have the project leader begin setting them up by the end of week four

6. Finish initial set up of profile pages by end of week six

7. Review advertising costs during process

Item 5 – Company Blog

1. Goal is to start a blog on our website week 6 of first quarter.

2. Ask the sales department and office staff to start it off beginning of week 3 and set aside a brainstorming time with coffee and donuts. Notify everyone of time and place.

3. Prepare a rough draft of the results, give to web manager by end of week four.

4. Get our web site manager to set up a page that allows interaction and show me how to look after it.

5. Post first blog week six.

6. Request entire staff for feed-back and suggestions.

Item 6 – Add Sales Representative

1. Add our first new sales representative to start approximately week 6 of first quarter.

2. Establish parameters of employment including remuneration type, benefits, sales targets

3. Begin advertising for this position immediately

4. Start final selection process by the end of week 3

5. Make selection end of week 4 to allow for 2 weeks' notice.

6. Research and purchase furniture and computer for sales rep. by week 4

Item 7 – Advertising and promotion

1. Begin advertising trial week 10 on social media sites

Summary Implementation Schedule Objectives First Quarter

Implementation Schedule can be set up as a list or in a spread sheet. Along with the spread sheet of objectives will be the first Quarter Budget to match these objectives.

First Quarter Sample Budget

Description	Budget Amount
Web site	
Design	$ 800
Support software	$ 00
Webinars	$ 00
Social Media	
Design	$ 800
Advertising	$ 350
Paid Traditional Advertising	
Trade shows	$ 00
Trade Publications	$ 00
Newspaper (help wanted)	$ 700
Other	$ 00
Internally generated	
Direct mail	$ 300
Office equipment and supplies	
Equipment, furniture	$1,800
Office supplies, brochures	$ 600
Client Maintenance	
Socializing, expense accounts	$ 600
Brand development	
Merchandising , promotions	$ 00
Educational Programs	
Morning meetings	$ 350
TOTAL	$6,300

Summary

CONGRATULATIONS YOU HAVE NOW COMPLETED

YOUR COMPANY'S MARKETING PLAN

Putting a marketing plan together is not easy and that is why so few people are willing to put in the effort to do one. When you are done, you will have an intimate knowledge of your company and be very much in control of your own destiny.

You will now be part of the 20% who have a marketing plan and you have now reached the tipping point between success and failure.

Your efforts have now created the process required to reach your goals and fulfill the reasons why you started your business in the first place.

Keep up the effort to review and renew your marketing plan every year as this is your model for success.

Wayne E Shillum - Author

www.ingramcontent.com/pod-product-compliance
Lightning Source LLC
Chambersburg PA
CBHW051221200326
41519CB00025B/7203